PRAISE FOR DR. ELAINE RUÍZ LÓPEZ AND *THE FIGHT FOR EQUITY IN THE BRONX*

Dr. Elaine Ruíz López speaks in an authentic voice supporting students struggling to keep up, encouraging advocates working in hard-pressed neighborhoods, as well as parents seeking inspiration for their children. Dr. López's lived experience will take you to her childhood Bronx block where you will feel the pulse of a struggling community in transition. Discover how the author could drop out of high school, get a GED, and then press on to get her Ph.D. Along the way, Dr. López earned national recognition from US News and World Report Bronze Award Recipient for Best High Schools for a school she developed. *The Fight for Equity In The Bronx: Changing Lives and Transforming Communities One Scholar at a Time* is a must read for social change agents, educators, academics, researchers, as well as individuals seeking examples of effective leadership.

—REVEREND DR. ALFONSO WYATT
Founder, Strategic Destiny: Designing Futures Through Faith and Facts

What an impactful book Dr. Elaine Ruíz López has written. I urge everyone who is involved in educating Black and Latinx children in places as rich as the South Bronx and similar communities throughout the country to read this book. *The Fight for Equity in the Bronx* is an inspirational account of the extraordinary challenges that this visionary and leader and woman of color confronted in order to provide a quality college prep high school education for Black and Brown children.

—MIRIAM RACCAH

Chief Executive Officer, Black Latinx Asian Charter Coalition (BLACC)

Dr. Elaine Ruíz López recounts her very storied life from humble beginnings as a child in the South Bronx through an astounding history of self-discovery. She describes how the school system failed her, the racism she experienced in her early years of teaching. We also get a glimpse of her community activism with National Congress of Puerto Rican Rights (NCPRR) led by former members of the Young Lords Party (YLP), which provided a platform for fighting for civil and human rights, education reform, and ultimately starting a school of choice in the Bronx. This compelling story is truly an inspiration for all aspiring Latinx leaders who are in the front lines for social justice and leading schools of choice in Black and Brown communities.

—DR. JOHN PAUL GONZALEZ GUTIERREZ

Adjunct Assistant Professor of Puerto Rican and Latino Studies, CUNY

Dr. Elaine chronicles her journey as a young, disempowered student to becoming a champion for high-quality education for all disenfranchised students. That journey has resulted in empowering hundreds of children's lives. This book is the story of the making of a champion."

—DR. VASHTI ACOSTA

Chief Executive Officer Emeritus, Amber Charter Schools

THE FIGHT FOR
EQUITY
IN THE
BRONX

THE FIGHT FOR

EQUITY

IN THE

BR★NX

**CHANGING LIVES AND
TRANSFORMING COMMUNITIES
ONE SCHOLAR AT A TIME**

DR. ELAINE RUÍZ LÓPEZ

Advantage | Books

Published by Advantage Books, Charleston, South Carolina.
An imprint of Advantage Media.

ADVANTAGE is a registered trademark, and the Advantage colophon is a trademark of Advantage Media Group, Inc.

Printed in the United States of America.

10 9 8 7 6 5 4 3 2 1

ISBN: 978-1-64225-731-1 (Hardcover)
ISBN: 978-1-64225-730-4 (eBook)

Library of Congress Control Number: 2024907664

Cover photography by Joe Conzo Jr. (bottom image)
Cover design by Matthew Morse.
Layout design by Megan Elger.

This publication is designed to provide accurate and authoritative information in regard to the subject matter covered. It is sold with the understanding that the publisher is not engaged in rendering legal, accounting, or other professional services. If legal advice or other expert assistance is required, the services of a competent professional person should be sought.

Advantage Books is an imprint of Advantage Media Group. Advantage Media helps busy entrepreneurs, CEOs, and leaders write and publish a book to grow their business and become the authority in their field. Advantage authors comprise an exclusive community of industry professionals, idea-makers, and thought leaders. For more information go to **advantagemedia.com**.

This book is dedicated to my husband and co-founder, Anthony López, who has supported me and the vision for the International Leadership Charter High School unconditionally from its inception.

Tony, I am grateful for your love, dedication, great home cooked meals, and always standing by me throughout all of the challenges and the rewards. This journey would not have been possible without you.

To my daughter, Monica, who was born to give my life meaning and purpose to pursue my education.

CONTENTS

BY DR. JOHN RODNEY JENKINS

My star crossed with Dr. Elaine Ruíz López's twenty-five years ago when we were both assistant principals on the leadership team of a high school in a small diverse suburban district located in Westchester County ten miles north of NYC. At the time, the schools were in chaos, and as administrators of color, we were both eyewitnesses and often the target of racial hostility and discrimination by members of the school board, the parents, teachers, and students. Many referred to this area as "up south."

We were told that our mission was to support the principal in turning around this school and to remove ineffective teachers who contributed to the failure of thousands of students of color. We were working to turn around a school's performance during a very significant civil rights battle to desegregate the district, which had violated a federal court order and failed to implement the federal mandate. The landmark desegregation case, filed by the National Association for the Advancement of Colored People (NAACP) and the Federal Court in 1980 and settled in 2007, found that city and school officials had purposefully segregated Black residents and students in public housing and schools.

In that moment, I had no idea how much our lives were already intertwined. We both were raised in the same four-mile radius of the South Bronx, the poorest congressional district in the country. We both experienced the phenomenon of being labeled "different" and "exceptional" by the public school system and as a result were distanced from our peers in ways that often led to ostracism. This is an experience that many bright students of color encounter as they are often forced to choose access to favor and quality education over being and learning with other students who look like them. From the moment that I met Elaine, it was clear that she was a fierce proponent of justice, equity, and access for students who confronted the same struggles we encountered in our journeys: the impact of poverty, exposure to violence, school cultures of low expectations, and limited access to the resources needed to inspire and motivate us to pursue our dreams. As members of an administration composed largely of people of color, we faced consistent challenges, as well as political and racial opposition as we tried to create change on behalf of a school population with a majority of Black and Brown students. As we battled the teachers' union, challenged a culture of mediocrity, and set high expectations for behavior and academic performance for students, I was able to experience Elaine demonstrate the confidence, courage, and commitment that would later serve as the undaunted spirit needed to create the International Leadership Charter High School (International Leadership CHS).

Although Elaine and I went our separate ways after that year together, we stayed connected as colleagues. I was a champion and supporter of Elaine's when she wrote the charter application and opened International Leadership CHS. I often sent words of prayer and comfort through the tumultuous first years chronicled in this book, when she and the new school were under attack. I had gone on to lead my own charter school in Fort Greene, Brooklyn, manage a network of high schools in NYC, and was serving as vice president of School Leaders Network, a national nonprofit that provided professional learning to principals across the country when Elaine reached out to make me an offer I would not refuse. In 2008, she invited me to join the board of International Leadership CHS and later take the role as board chair. As board chair, my role was to stand beside Elaine and the other members of the International Leadership CHS Board to form a protective hedge around the school at all costs. We knew how incredibly important the school was and would continue to be to this community, and we had to be relentless in our protection of the leader, the staff, and the students. I was never unclear about that calling and I never questioned my role and my purpose in that regard. Elaine chronicles the deliberate actions we took to ensure our school was successful. She provides key insight into what a board looks like when it is truly invested in creating an innovative, uncharted experience for students. A board is tasked not only with governance but also with advocacy and protection of the integrity and autonomy of the institution. The four years I spent as Board Chair of International Leadership CHS were some of the most rewarding years of my personal and professional life. I will always be proud and incredibly thankful to the friend, colleague, and change maker who invited me along for the journey.

In this book, Elaine illustrates the inextricable relationship between lived experience and leadership. She provides a gripping portrait of her early life growing up in the Bronx and details how that experience shaped her but did not deter her from success. Her journey from a gifted and talented elementary school student to signing out of high school without graduating demonstrates the inconsistent and fragile nature of the school system of NYC. She also recounts the challenges of becoming a teen mother and thus needing to shift her attention to the responsibilities of life that most teenagers do not need to consider. Life presented many challenges for Elaine that unfortunately were common among her peers growing up in the South Bronx. Her story does not, however, end there. The decision and ability to earn her General Equivalency Diploma (GED) and attend City College placed Elaine on the trajectory to change not only her life but also the lives of the many children she would go on to touch as an educator. Indeed, Elaine's lived experience was a testament to the transformative power of education, especially for people of color living in communities of poverty. This lived experience was the fire and foundation that would help this determined young woman to persevere through one of her most significant contributions, the founding of the International Leadership CHS.

The book is simultaneously a leadership road map, an inspirational memoir, a model of community activism, and a story of a political movement. In it, Elaine details why she was compelled to open a rigorous, high-performing high school for students of color in the Bronx and shares in a clear transparent fashion all the oppositions and obstacles she faced along the way. As a visionary and strategic leader, she had the uncanny ability to predict the moves of the opposition, whether they came from the NY State charter authorizer, the New York City Department of Education (NYCDOE), a group of misinformed community members, partisan public officials, or disgruntled former staff members. She was able to rally the parent and student community, engage the board members, and leverage external support and advocates to push back against rumors, overstepping of authority, and attempts to deny the school access to vital resources.

She simply did not accept no for an answer, when it came to our quest to build a pillar of excellence in the Bronx. This book details how she defended the dream she had for Bronx children, spoke truth to power, and stood in the face of one mounting Goliath after the next.

In my thirty-three years as an educator, I have had the joy of serving as a teacher, school leader, facilitator, and executive coach across the education, nonprofit, and corporate sectors. I have never been more inspired and called to action in the work I do than I am at this moment in time. In my role as a leader of a national nonprofit I am devoted to creating equity-focused leaders who transform schools and the trajectories of Black and Brown children. My mission is to replicate leaders like Elaine across the country. We seek to change the trajectory for students who live and learn in places like the Bronx community where Elaine and I were born and raised. This book serves as a guide for entrepreneurial leaders, community organizers, school administrators, and district and charter management organization (CMO) leaders who desire to disrupt historical patterns of under-achievement and limited access for students of color in the public education space. It is also an intimate and personal tale for young Black and Brown people who are not sure what their mission in life is or who believe the cards they have been dealt can't be used to win the game. The story of Dr. Elaine Ruíz López and the International Leadership CHS is a strong affront to those who believe that will, determination, and courage are insufficient to overcome the unre-lenting weight of poverty and racism. You will be inspired, informed, and empowered by this story. Most importantly, you will be activated to drive yourselves, your communities, and your colleagues to reach beyond their work to the world and achieve true change, transforma-tion, and impact for the sake of humanity.

T he outline for the first three chapters of this book was completed during the height of the coronavirus pandemic in New York State, a highly contagious and dangerous virus that contributed to the illness and death of over thirteen thousand of its residents at the first writing of this chapter and over twenty-five thousand by May of 2020. The introduction to this book would be incomplete without memorializing the experience of the first national disaster and public health crisis in a century caused by COVID-19. Not since the Spanish Flu of 1918 has the world experienced such horrific loss of life and a global threat that would close down our schools, businesses, churches; separate families at the end of life; and change our lives and hold the world hostage.

On March 18, 2020, it was clear that all schools in New York State would have to close and that our operations, business, school finances, and academic program would all be conducted from our homes. The New York State Governor Cuomo issued an Executive Order through March 31, 2020. By May 15, 2020, this order would be extended at least three more times, ultimately prohibiting the return of over two million students to the classroom and indefinitely closing schools statewide.

In this inspirational memoir, I begin by taking the reader to a glimpse of my life and education as a Puerto Rican child in the South Bronx, highlighting many of the struggles and the socioeconomic circumstances that I was born into, educated, and raised in. The challenges and events that I experienced would later spark my drive to become an educator, a civil rights and community activist, and to change the trajectory of Puerto Rican/Latino youth and all children of color and the communities that they lived in. Woven into the background of all chapters is my passionate pursuit of justice in the systems, institutions, and bureaucracies that are steeped in a history of serving those who are privileged based on their race and class.

In chapters 1–3, I provide a snapshot of a poor working-class migrant and immigrant community on Simpson Street where I lived up to the age of thirteen. Public School 20 was the elementary school that I attended, right across the street from the 41st Precinct that would later be featured in a racist movie named Fort Apache featuring Paul Newman. The police officers treated Puerto Ricans as spics, prostitutes, and criminals. In the upper grades, I would walk alone in the morning and in the afternoons run home past drug dealers, sexual predators, and burned-out buildings. The landlords would come to the door to collect rent in cash from my father. I highlight my journey from an elementary and secondary school education, to being "*pushed out*" of high school, to becoming pregnant by someone who was a dropout and a heroin addict. I was a child having a child and struggled as a teenage mom, never quite meeting the expectations thrust upon me and then found my way to becoming a college student at the City College of New York (CCNY). This decision to pursue this opportunity would ultimately change my life and put me on a path toward becoming a teacher in the same neighborhood where I was raised.

In chapters 4–7, I take the reader to my early years of teaching during the latter part of when the Bronx was burning, the arson and decade of fire. The same fires led my parents to take their family and flee from Simpson Street in 1970. I provide a snapshot of the hostility and the racism that I experienced as a young teacher. I also talk about meeting one of my "*heroes*" and one who gave me the inspiration to build a school, the mother of the South Bronx, Dr. Evelina Lopez Antonetty. She taught me about speaking truth to power and modeled how to fight for my rights and that of my community.

In chapters 8–11, the reader will journey through my graduate and postgraduate school experience, the microaggressions I encountered, and how I became part of the "less than 2 percent" when I became an Ivy League student at Teachers College (TC), Columbia University. Then I will recount how I earned my doctorate and how I developed my vision for equity in education for children in the Bronx.

In chapters 12–15, I take the reader to 2004 and my perspective on the politics of educational reform and starting a charter school in NYC, and the obstacles that were intentionally placed in our way so that we would fail, to the journey to opening our charter school, and the battle to keep our school opened and thriving.

In chapters 16–20, I bring the reader to a decade later when our vision was fulfilled, winning the battle to keep our charter school open and exposing the NYC Chancellor's Charter Schools Office and the New York State Education Department (NYSED) for its deliberate attempts to sabotage and to interfere with our charter agreement. If successful, this would have impacted the thousands of children of color whom we have educated over the past seventeen years. With widespread parenting and community support, we expanded. In 2016 we moved into a brand new school with the assistance of investors who purchased $21 million bond to support our charter school with the financing of the construction. In the fall of 2023, we opened a middle school that was approved by our authorizers State University of New York Charter Schools Institute (SUNY CSI) and with the support of the Walton Family Foundation. At present, our charter school is highly regarded and recognized for its consistent achievement record, sending more than 95 percent of its graduates to the college of their choice. The school has been recognized and ranked by US NEWS & WORLD REPORT and cited among the Best High Schools locally and nationally and among the Best Charter Schools in the Bronx and NYC. We have been able to close the achievement gap for thousands of young people from the Bronx.

CHAPTER 1

YOUNG, GIFTED, AND PUERTO RICAN: MY CHILDHOOD IN THE SOUTH BRONX

> "I was born and raised in the South Bronx, the poorest congressional district in the country and in fact, poorer than the state of Mississippi."
>
> **—DR. ELAINE RUÍZ LÓPEZ**

was born on April 12, 1956, at the original Lincoln Hospital in the Bronx that was previously named "*The Colored Home and Hospital.*"

My mother would often share the story of the day that she went into labor during a spring snowstorm. Approximately twenty inches of snow had fallen two weeks prior. Mami was a beautiful dark-skinned Puerto Rican *mulatta* woman of African and Spaniard ancestry.. She shared with me that because I was born light skinned with rosy cheeks, the nurse had given her a dark baby instead of me. Apparently, I was

Old Lincoln Hospital

temporarily given to another woman with a lighter complexion. On my Birth Certificate my mother's race was listed as "colored." Fortunately, *Mami* recalled seeing me when I was born and knew that the nurse had not brought the right child to her.

This hospital had a very bad reputation and was locally referred to as the "Butcher Shop." It would be fourteen years later when on July 14, 1970, the Young Lords Party (YLP), a group of Puerto Rican community activists, would take over Lincoln Hospital, in protest against its substandard healthcare and mistreatment of the Puerto Rican communities' healthcare needs. They made demands for accessible quality healthcare for all.[1] The YLP activists were inspired by the student movements in Puerto Rico and by the Black Panther Party[2] that fought for community control of institutions and highlighting institutional failures. The Lincoln Hospital takeover by the YLP[3] gave rise to a movement to eradicate tuberculosis in poor communities and the first *Patients' Bill of Rights* in the country.[4] It would take another

---

1   Emma Francis-Snyder, "The hospital occupation that changed public health care," https://www.nytimes.com/2021/10/12/opinion/young-lords-nyc-activism-takeover.html.

2   Iris Morales, *Through the Eyes of Rebel Women: The Young Lords 1969-1976* (New York: Red Sugarcane Press, 2016).

3   Felipe Luciano, *Flesh and Spirit: Confessions of a Young Lord* (Empire State Editions, 2023).

4   Johanna Fernandez, *The Young Lords: A Radical History* (Chapel Hill: University of North Carolina Press, 2022).

six years for a new Lincoln Hospital to be constructed on 149th Street off of the Grand Concourse.

At that time, the Bronx was a quiet, safe, working-class borough, where children played kickball in the street, johnny the pony, and hot peas and butter. Little did I know as a young child the changes that would impact my life over the years to come. The quality of life in the Bronx took a sharp decline during the mid-1960s to the mid-1970s. In addition to the high poverty rate, crime, gangs, and a heroin epidemic, the borough was plagued by a wave of arson. The torching of buildings while families slept was commonplace during that time in the South Bronx. Many landlords decided to pay gang members or junkies to set their properties on fire, in a cruel and greedy plan to collect insurance money.

Our family was burned out of two of the three buildings where we lived on Simpson Street. The Bronx was burning with human beings inside, who had nowhere to go. It was a very frightening and traumatizing period in my childhood and that of my siblings. These scary experiences were not discussed, unpacked, or explained to us by our parents. Later as a college student, I learned that these social economic conditions also contributed

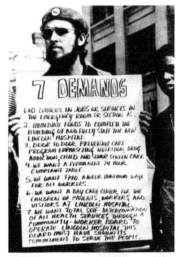

Photo credit: Michael Abramson, Courtesy of Haymarket Books

Young Lords Party Logo. Palante 2, no. 4 June 5, 1970; Courtesy of Tamiment Library

to the low expectations and "blame the victim" mentality that was all too prevalent in the education system.

¡Palante Siempre Palante! The Young Lords. Courtesy of P.O.V. Youth Views, Outreach Tool Kit That Accompanies Film produced and Directed, by former Young Lord, Iris Morales. From upper left Juan Gonzalez, David Perez, Juan "Fi" Ortiz, Pablo Yoruba Guzman, Denise Oliver

I faced my first challenge as a Puerto Rican child attending an elementary school in the 1960s in the South Bronx on Simpson Street. This was right across the street from the 41st Precinct renamed "Fort Apache"—a derogatory term coined by law enforcement for the neighborhood. The people who lived in this community were predominantly Puerto Rican and African American families. I recall running into the lobby of the precinct a few times after school to shine my Buster Brown shoes on a huge shine brush that was always turning for the officers' use. My mother would watch from the outside while I would happily run in to the laughter of the cops inside.

I recall a small hill on the alleyway between the precinct and the adjacent building, where children would run to after school in the winter to sit either on a piece of cardboard or the metal scrap from a refrigerator, to slide down the hill after a snowfall. This was one of the few moments of joy that I remember as a very young child.

However, I was unaware that these men in blue were involved in terrorizing our community. In the summer, the neighborhood families would gather in the schoolyard at P.S. 20. When the cops wanted to disperse the crowds, they would shoot their guns in the air and everyone would run up the street screaming. During one of these instances, I was with my mother and ran as fast as I could with my heart thumping, and I fell and scraped my knees. I was frightened and crying. When we reached our building a neighbor who was at her window on the first floor noticed that I was very agitated, and she gave me a cup of water. From that moment on, I did not feel safe. Who were they shooting at and why? This hostile and violent behavior was going on for some time before I was born. Kerry Washington, Bronx native and actress, started a podcast named "Simpson Street." She conducted an interview with her mom, now Dr. Valerie Washington, about attending the elementary school P.S. 20. This is the same elementary school that I attended a decade after she did. She asked Dr. Washington about the feelings that she had about the police being on her block. The police precinct was directly across the street from the school.

Kerry asks "Did it make you feel safe?" Dr. Washington replies:

"They were not kind to the boys who played stick ball. For some reason, they found it necessary to take the boys' bats and break them… so that history of antagonism goes back quite a ways, even if it is not as overt as it may be today. I don't know where or what neighborhoods the police came from other than the suburbs that exist like they do today… but they were clearly not from the South Bronx."

Dr. Washington, now in her late eighties, resonates with me as she became a teacher after graduating from Hunter College and taught in the South Bronx and later became a professor at the college level.[5] In 1976, the racist stereotypes were further perpetuated by a book

---

5   Lynsey Eidell, "All about Kerry Washington's parents, Valerie and Earl Washington," https://people.com/all-about-kerry-washington-parents-7975505.

written by Tom Walker, a police officer at the 41st Precinct on Simpson Street. The title of the book was *Fort Apache: New York's Most Violent Precinct.*[6] The setting took place on the very street where I was born and raised. The book would subsequently be made into a very-low-rate movie in 1981 by the same name of "*Fort Apache*" starring Paul Newman.

41st Precinct

Much later in my thirties, while in graduate school, I channeled a lot of my anger and outrage at the injustices in the Puerto Rican community by joining a Puerto Rican civil rights organization. I became an activist and learned how to become outspoken, and about the mechanics of how to organize and fight for the rights of my people. I participated in a myriad of protests organized by the Committee Against Fort Apache[7] composed of educators and civil rights activists from the National Congress for Puerto Rican Rights (NCPRR). We marched in front of NBC Studios against the showing of this movie and the shameful racist exploitation of the producers who depicted our families and our people in this terrible way.[8]

---

6   Tom Walker, Fort Apache: New York's Most Violent Precinct (New York: Crowell, 1976).

7   "The Committee Against Fort Apache," Cornell University Department of History, accessed November 25, 2022, https://phi.history.cornell.edu/projects/archival-finds/the-committee-against-fort-apache/.; "NCPRR: New York City," Robert M. Farnsworth, accessed November 25, 2022, https://www.columbia.edu/~rmg36/ncprr_ny/ncprr_ny.html.

8   "Fort Apache Archives," Media and Social Justice History Project at Hampshire College, accessed November 25, 2022, https://www.mediajusticehistoryproject.org/archives/82.

In the late 1960s, the area's population began decreasing because of new policies demanding that in order to create racial balance in schools, children would be bused into other districts. Parents who worried about their children attending school outside their district often relocated to the suburbs, where this was not a concern. In addition, rent control policies are thought to have contributed to the decline of many middle-class neighborhoods in the 1950s and 1960s; New York City's policies regarding rent control gave building owners no motivation to keep up their properties. Therefore, desirable housing options were scarce, and vacancies further increased. By the time the city decided to consolidate welfare households in the South Bronx, its vacancy rate was already the highest of any place in the city.

The South Bronx has historically been a place for working-class families. Later, it gained an image of a poverty-ridden area that was developed in the latter part of the twentieth century. There have been several factors contributing to the

Photos by Joe Conzo, Jr

Photo by Joe Conzo, Jr

decay of the South Bronx from the 1960s through the 1980s: white flight, landlord abandonment, changes in economic demographics, and the construction of the Cross Bronx Expressway.

In the 1950s, thousands of Puerto Ricans flew north to the United States for the promise of a better life and improved economic conditions for their families. This postwar period in the history of Puerto Ricans migrating to the United States was referred to as the "great migration."[9] A project named "Operation Bootstrap" was essentially an economic recovery plan that was led by Luis Munoz Marin, who became the first governor of Puerto Rico after catapulting Puerto Rico into a commonwealth status with the United States in 1952. This was a well-orchestrated plan between the United States and the island's government. According to the Center for Puerto Rican Studies at Hunter College,[10] this economic plan was a result of the shift from an agrarian economy to an industrial one. The implementation of

---

9   https://centropr-archive.hunter.cuny.edu/education/story-us-puerto-ricans-part-four.

10   https://centropr-archive.hunter.cuny.edu/education/learning-unit-9-industrialization-and-progress-manos-la-obra-operation-bootstrap.

this economic plan meant that a third of the island's Puerto Rican population would be encouraged to migrate north to the mainland. This was intended to alleviate the crushing poverty on the island and to give an economic boost to the mainland that had suffered post-World War II labor shortages.

Eighty-five percent of those who migrated settled in New York City, and both of my parents were among them. My parents were among thousands who traveled for six hours on repurposed military cargo war planes that were outfitted with wooden benches and lawn chairs bolted to the floor of the plane. The flight was described by

Alfonso Ruíz Martinez

Abuelo Juan Ruíz Torres

Mami Ventura Martinez

Tia Conrada Martinez, my grand-aunt

Mama Bernarda Martinez, my great grandmother

Tia Fela Ruíz, my aunt

both of them as a frightening and a grueling trip.

My father, Alfonso Ruíz Martinez, was a very proud and hard-working Puerto Rican man who was fiercely loyal and protective of his family. Like most *puertorriqueños,* he was of mixed race and heritage. My grandmother *Mami Ventura* was indigenous of Taino and Spanish heritage that is traced back to the Canary Islands off the coast of North Africa. My grandfather Juan Ruíz Torres was of a Spanish Lineage—he raised a family of eight. At the age of nineteen, my father migrated to the United States from Ponce, Puerto Rico, and settled in the South Bronx in 1952. His aunt, Tia Conrada Martinez, was born in 1919 in Penuelas, Puerto Rico. Tia Conrada would become the matriarch for his side of the family stateside, hosting my father and several of his siblings, who were searching for a better life and greater economic opportunities in the United States.

My grand aunt, Tia Conrada, migrated to New York in 1950. She settled on 851 Prospect Avenue in the South Bronx. She hosted my father, two of his sisters, Lola and Rafaela, and eldest brother, Francisco nicknamed "Pancho." For several years Mama Bernarda Martinez, my paternal great-grandmother, traveled to the Bronx from Ponce, Puerto Rico, and lived with her daughter on Prospect Avenue to take care of her grandchildren while she worked. Tia Conrada was described as a very strict, hard-working, and caring aunt who although had children of her own looked after the well-being of her nieces and nephews. She worked as a seamstress in the fashion district. My aunt Tia Fela (Rafaela), now eighty-seven, was one of the nieces who lived with her in Bronx, New York. With a lot of tenderness and gratitude in her voice, Tia Fela recalls that as a young girl in Puerto Rico, the family would receive packages with beautiful clothing that were all handmade by Tia Conrada, for her and her siblings. It was these handmade clothes lovingly made by her Tia that she would wear on the day that she took the grueling six-hour flight to New York in 1952 to begin a new life.

My mother, Lucila Rodriguez Ortiz, also traveled from Guayanilla, Puerto Rico, in 1952 to the Bronx under the same circumstances. Mami traveled from San Juan airport with a one-way ticket on May 15, 1952, on Eastern Airlines for $64.00. She left two children from her first tumultuous marriage behind with her sister Aileen and her mother, Mama Zenobia, who was lovingly referred to as *Yaya*. Mami made this painful sacrifice in pursuit of a better

Mami, Guayanilla, Puerto Rico

life for her and her children and to escape poverty. She relied a great deal on the support of her aunt, Tia Carmela, who had arrived in New York in the late 1940s and was able to guide her and open doors to factories where she could work as a seamstress. My parents met in the South Bronx. They fell in love and married in 1954. Mami met my father while living on Stebbins Avenue and they were later married in a civil ceremony on April 28, 1954.

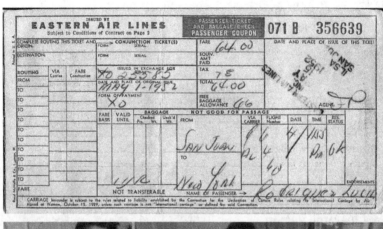

1954 Civil Wedding

My father would leave to work in the wee hours of the morning to toil at the iron and steel factories in the Hunts Point area, which at the time was one of the most corrupt and violent areas of the Bronx, controlled by organized crime. It was referred to as the "red light district." I recall that he would arrive home at night, visibly agitated and frustrated from the long hours, as well as the intense labor for menial wages and the abuse that he experienced from racist supervisors. The challenges of raising a large family in the South Bronx during the 1960s were daunting. It was his job to provide a decent home, food on the table, appropriate school clothing, and to keep us all safe in one of the most corrupt and violent areas of the Bronx.

My mother Lucila was left to manage a household of five children. Three were under the age of six and two were my teenage half-siblings from my mother's previous marriage in Puerto Rico before she began her new life in New York. By 1966, there would be two additions to the family and a household of seven children to support and raise to adulthood. However, the hardships that she endured as a child and adolescent in Puerto Rico would prepare her for the harsh reality of living in the South Bronx while Puerto Rican.

LUCILA RODRIGUEZ ORTIZ: SURVIVOR OF LA MASSACRE DE PONCE

Later in my journey, one of the courses I took at CCNY was on the history of Latin America, Puerto Rico, and the Caribbean. This and the Puerto Rican civil rights organization that I joined, where I was introduced to *"sociopolitical education and consciousness raising topics"* gave me greater insight into the history of Puerto Ricans and who we are as a people and nation. This is where I would forge an identity and understanding of my heritage and a deep awareness of our family history. I would come home to share with *Mami* what I had learned about the colonization of Puerto Ricans, and that we were able to become citizens as a result of the 1917 Jones Act. I had conversations with her about the brutality of colonization at the hands of the Spanish conquistadores, the subhuman treatment of African slaves, and the annihilation of the indigenous people who are also part of our DNA. I would passionately share what I learned about the US invasion of 1898.

Up to that point, I had never heard her mention our African ancestry beyond the obvious, that her mother and siblings were Black. I passionately told her that there were Africans who were brought to Puerto Rico as slaves. Up to that point she was still resisting any connection to her roots. Mami, at the age of five, after my grandfather Rosario Urutia Bosch Rodriguez passed away in 1929, spent most of her time with her aunt *Carmen Ortiz Medina* (*Tia Carmela*) and uncle *Tio Quino* in Ponce, one of the larger *pueblos* on the island. My grand

My grand-aunt, Tia Carmela and her husband, Jose Medina

aunt *Tia Carmela* had served as one of the nurses and a member of "*las Cadetas de la Republica*" in the nationalist party along with her husband. They were Puerto Rican nationalists and followers of Don Pedro Albizu Campos, "*El Maestro*." He was an Afro-Boricua attorney who graduated from Harvard Law School in the early 1930s. He enlisted as a soldier in World War I. Don Pedro was a brilliant intellectual and orator. He dedicated his life to the independence of Puerto Rico and decolonization from the United States. He was to Puerto Rico what Nelson

Mandela was to South Africa, a freedom fighter, revolutionary, and nationalist.

When I came to the part of *"La Massacre de Ponce"* in 1937, she became animated and reflective. She began to speak with intention and with great detail and quietly shared that she and her siblings, aunt and uncle who were her guardians at the time were survivors of *"La Massacre."* I sat and listened in disbelief and awe that my mother had lived through and survived this part of our history. Mami shared in vivid detail about Palm Sunday morning on March 21, 1937, in Ponce, Puerto Rico, when the nationalists gathered in *"La Plaza de las Delicias."* They all attended a church service. She described how under the leadership of Don Pedro there were plans for a peaceful march to commemorate the abolition of slavery, and to declare Puerto Rico as a sovereign nation that was seeking its independence from colonization and oppression of the US government. After they reached Calle Aurora y Calle Marina, Don Pedro and other leaders made speeches and then the march would begin with the singing of *"La Borinquena,"* the National Anthem of Puerto Rico.

She was a witness to this history, right down to telling me all the details of the white dresses that the *enfermeras* wore, the male cadet uniforms that consisted of white pants and black shirts, the anthem that they would start to sing, and how her younger brother (my uncle) Tio Reinaldo Ortiz Rodriguez was in the front of the marchers and was one of the bearers of the Puerto Rican flag. Reinaldo, who was ten years of age, was positioned in front of the march. Mami, with tears in her eyes, recalled that when the nationalist anthem began and my uncle, my

mother, and her sisters took a few steps and began marching, they heard gunshots. The crowd, screaming and crying, dispersed and went running in different directions. Over two hundred police officers called in from various towns for reinforcement carrying rifles and bayonets opened fire. The nationalists were unarmed. I was in shock for a few days and could not believe that she did not share

Source: Library of Congress, Prints & Photographs Division, Farm Security Administration/Office of War Information Black-and-White Negatives.

this before. I could not wait to share with my friends about this history. I went back to my textbooks on Puerto Rican history and my fact-checking and research would support all the details of Mami's eyewitness accounts. There were hundreds wounded and seventeen nationalists murdered, including innocent children who were massacred, along with two police officers. Among the dead was one of my mother's classmates who was twelve, Georgina Maldonado who died with Palm Sunday fronds in her hands. Years later I would visit the site of the massacre to find her name on the commemorative plaque.

It is a well-documented fact that there were orders by General Blanton Winship that if the nationalists did not abandon their plans to march, they would be threatened with violence. An assistant to the governor, at Fortaleza (the Governor's Mansion), decided that the parade was military in character and therefore illegal. The police on site had orders to "shoot to kill" if they disobeyed the order. Mami recollected that the whereabouts of my uncle Tio Rey were unknown for a few hours. Oral histories as told by my mother and uncle and also collected by his daughters (my cousins) tell how he hid under a dead body for a while and then freed himself and ran to a nearby house, where he pushed the door open, and there he and others were able to take refuge.[11]

Years later in the late 1990s, I would visit the site that is a landmark building now turned into a museum. "*El Museo de La Massacre de Ponce*" is situated at the very corner where "*La Massacre*" took place and the building where Don Pedro and the nationalist headquarters would conduct their meetings, plan, and organize their strategies to obtain independence. The police were never charged with a crime despite the eyewitnesses and evidence that the nationalists were unarmed. Blanton Winship was removed from office by President Roosevelt in 1939.

It was no coincidence that with the knowledge of this part of my mother's history that I discovered in my late twenties, I found myself and several of my maternal cousins drawn to revolutionary ideals and radical causes, to fight for the independence of Puerto Rico and for social and economic justice. The spirit of resistance was in our DNA. It was only natural that my mother's trauma of 1937 would make

---

11   Democracynow, "Remembering Puerto Rico's Ponce Massacre," March 22, 2007, https://www.democracynow.org/2007/3/22/remembering_puerto_ricos_ ponce_massacre.

her fearful of my participation in numerous marches and protests that I would join defending the rights of Puerto Ricans against police brutality, inadequate housing and healthcare, and a quality education for all. I never stopped fighting.

ELEMENTARY SCHOOL: P.S. 20

In 1962, my parents registered me in kindergarten at Public School 20, one-and-a-half blocks from where we lived on Simpson Street. I recall my elementary school as being very structured and well-disciplined. The building was already fifty years old and spacious, with at least sixty thousand square feet and a gymnasium and a very large schoolyard. The school had five floors filled with classrooms that were furnished with wooden student desks with a space for inkwells, black slate chalkboards, closet space, and a very large wooden teacher's desk.

In this environment, it was clear that the adults were in charge. Our principal, Mr. Lonoff, and assistant principal, Ms. Larkin, were very strict and businesslike. All of them were white. The teachers were always well-groomed, with a professional appearance and prepared to teach. It was only much later that I became aware that the teachers there had very low expectations for Puerto Rican children like me. Apparently I was one of the exceptions, and some of my teachers took notice of my academic achievements and potential.

Public School 20, Bronx

COMMENDATION CARD

Elaine Ruiz of

Class ___5-1___ is hereby commended for excellence

in ___School work___

Date ___22, 1967___ RICHARD LONOFF, Principal

I was enrolled into classes for the gifted students otherwise known as the Intellectually Gifted Child (IGC) program. I did not realize it then, but I was being "tracked." I was seated in the front of the class and could pick out as many books as I was interested in reading. I was also given special privileges such as becoming the class monitor and running errands for my fifth- and sixth-grade teachers, bringing them tuna fish sandwiches and stockings. I was among a group of "favorite" students, the "teacher's pet" who filled the basin with water to wash the chalkboards clean and got to sit up front and close to my teacher's desk. This is an attribute that later came into view quite differently, once I started my career in teaching and understood the implications for other children like me who survived the stereotypes and unequal treatment.

I always brought home excellent marks for each of the four quarters of my report cards for the years that I attended grades 1–6. The only comment that displeased my parents was that I was very talkative. Due to my high achievement, I was rewarded by the librarian to serve as a volunteer in the school library. My job was to cover the hardcover books in clear plastic jackets for protection. I enjoyed this task and knew I was doing something important for the education of others. I loved the way the books would feel in my hands and how they were illustrated.

As a child, I would often randomly walk into a library on Southern Boulevard on the way home, just to look at the books and imagine all the knowledge that was found inside of the pages. There was a sense of peace and solace in the library that I never experienced anywhere else during those elementary school years. This practice and love of books continued well into my college years at CCNY as well as graduate school and carried into my early years of teaching and throughout my entire professional life.

My parents were informed at every parent teacher conference that I was different—very smart, with very high reading and language skills, despite the fact that neither of them spoke English well, they understood the language as they were both required to take English courses in Puerto Rico. I was characterized as having great academic potential and promise of becoming the first female astronaut. They were told that I could do anything that I set my mind on. By the time that I was in the sixth grade, I was reading at an eleventh-grade level. The IGC classes that I was enrolled in were designated as Special Progress Classes from the first through seventh grade. Although I was on a "Special Progress" track, what I will always recall vividly is the huge disappointment and sense of failure I felt, as I did not consider myself well prepared enough to take a special-

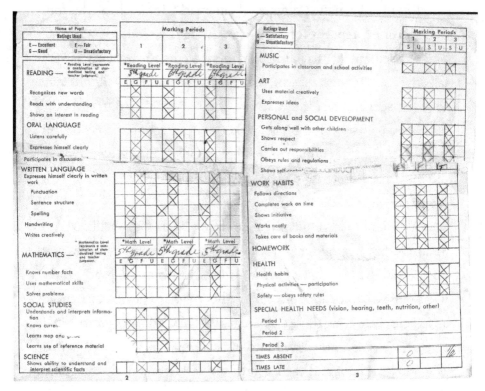

My Fifth Grade Report Card

ized exam for admission into the highly specialized and very competitive program I hoped to enter.

I was one of a handful of students from my fifth-grade class who were selected to take a specialized exam for admission to Hunter College Junior High School on the east side of New York City. But I was so poorly prepared for this assessment that I left most of my exam page blank—specifically in mathematics. Even though I was excelling academically at P.S. 20, it was clear that I was not being prepared to compete for a seat at a specialized school. This would have required acceleration in the mathematics curriculum that I was exposed to, which was above the level that I was learning.

I did not have the same equal preparation and opportunity to succeed at this examination, although I was selected among four other female students in the fifth grade due to high scores in English and reading. This select group of students were representative of Puerto Rican, Irish, and Jewish heritage. I was favored and well-liked by my teachers in the upper grades and my academic achievement reflected "excellent" marks noted on all report cards. The comments demonstrated that reading was my favorite activity and that I had the potential of becoming the first female astronaut. These observations and comments thrilled my parents and made them very proud. I was their shining star. However, performing very well at a school in the South Bronx was not enough. I was not fully prepared for the rigor of a highly specialized examination, and the window of opportunity that was being afforded to me closed, and as a result I received a failing grade. I remember the moment that I was informed that I was no longer being considered for this prestigious program of study. My head hung down with disappointment. I was devastated. I later learned that only one of my four classmates who took the exam passed and was selected for special entrance to the private secondary school.

CHAPTER 2

FROM SHINING STAR
TO DIMMING LIGHT

> "My life growing up was a twisted Bronx version of
> *The Color Purple*. It had a much different soundtrack
> and no trees, but that desperation was the same."
> **—TRACY MORGAN**

Middle School Transition: Becoming a casualty of tracking

Professor Robert E. Slavin[12] explains that the practice of tracking began in the 1930s and has been the subject of intense scrutiny and criticism for the past thirty years. It is a method used by many to group students according to their perceived ability, IQ, or achievement levels. Students are placed in high, middle, or low tracks, to provide them with a level of curriculum and instruction that is appropriate to their individual needs. This model is believed to be inequitable and damaging to students, par-

---

12   Robert E. Slavin, "Achievement Effects of Ability Grouping in Secondary Schools: A Best Evidence Synthesis," *Review of Educational Research* 60, no. 3 (Fall 1990): 471–499.

ticularly from low and middle tracks where there are predominantly low-income or poor students of color.

According to the Education Trust[13] (2004), the education of students on the lower tracks emphasizes socialization, positive behaviors, and the acquisition of menial skills. Historically, these students are typically assigned the least qualified teachers; the best and most effective teachers are reserved for students who are in the high-achieving track. This model institutionalizes a system for failure for the students on the "low-achieving" track, and disparate performance for students on the "high-achieving" track as compared with those on a "low-achieving" track.

In junior high school, I experienced what I will refer to as "reverse tracking." This is a process in which secondary schools sift through the questionable performance of students and without much thought or consideration for the child's history of high academic achievement, there is a decision to demote students from a higher track to a lower track. After being placed in classes for the IGC student for all six years of elementary school, I was reassigned to a "lower achievement" track in seventh grade due to poor performance and over seventy chronic absences. I was referred to see a counselor, who would analyze and observe me to determine what was wrong with me.

I could not and would not speak for a long period of time and felt no joy. As I look back, I believe I was suffering from a severe depression that was recurring through my adolescence. But the depression was not diagnosed. The meeting with the counseling psychologist was unsuccessful, and it was determined that I would be demoted to another track.

---

13 Education Watch New York. Key Education Facts and Figures. Achievement, Attainment and Opportunity from Elementary School Through College. 2004.

The school system failed me, just as it did to thousands of countless and nameless others. For over seventy years, the practice of tracking in middle schools has been a subject of great debate. More recently, the topic of tracking students in accordance with their ability group has undergone great scrutiny. For the past thirty years, there has been a push to move from the model of homogeneous to heterogeneous instruction as a path toward leveling the playing field for poor students of color, and to ensure that all students are provided the same curriculum and level of instruction that other children would receive. In a homogeneous model, all students would be of the same or similar ability and skills, whereas in a heterogeneous model, students of diverse ability

THE SCHOOL SYSTEM FAILED ME, JUST AS IT DID TO THOUSANDS OF COUNTLESS AND NAMELESS OTHERS.

and skill sets would be exposed to the same curriculum and resources and learn in the same class.[14] The research supports that this would increase equity in education, offer greater opportunities for students of color to succeed, and eliminate bias inherent in predetermining which students will read the classics, which students will be taught an accelerated science and mathematics curriculum, and who will be prepared to attend college.

According to Professor Robert E. Slavin,[15] this form of tracking by ability grouping and by classrooms "has no benefits for anyone." Professor Slavin has conducted extensive research that shows that this practice will only benefit those students who are already high achieving and will hurt students of color from poor communities

14 Debra Viadero, "Research on tracking," October 14, 1998, https://www.edweek.org/education/research-on-tracking/1998/09.

15 Laura Manserus, "Should tracking be derailed?" November 1, 1992, https://www.nytimes.com/1992/11/01/education/should-tracking-be-derailed.html.

who are already marginalized. He states that "the segregation of these students has a negative impact on their behaviors, social-development, and further limits their opportunities and prospects for post-secondary education."

The ongoing and consistent attempts to provide me with social emotional support would have revealed that I was experiencing adolescent trauma due to domestic violence in the home, as well as the presence of sexual predators in our extended family and community. The escalating demise of the neighborhood and the torching of buildings on the street where we lived added to the trauma. This experience was further exacerbated with the rampant heroin use and addiction all around us, right at the footsteps of our building, and on the rooftops of the three buildings where we lived. I was terrified.

Two of my younger brothers had special needs and their behaviors were extremely challenging. Apparently, my mother did not notice my problems, as she was busy managing a house of five children, nor did she know how to provide me support since she was overwhelmed by her own challenges as a mother and wife. The presumption was that I was the high-performing child who had the most success and the least problems, so the supervision was not there. This made me more vulnerable and left me to figure everything out on my own at ten to thirteen years of age, and I did not receive the support I needed.

I was removed from the Special Progress track at the end of the seventh grade and placed into a middle-level track to a French and orchestra class (8-FO2). I barely learned how to play the upright bass and my understanding of French is limited to the greetings and the basic vocabulary to survive if ever ordering in a French restaurant or needed to use a restroom. This was the beginning of a downward spiral in my educational experience.

When it was time for high school, I was clearly tracked to a vocational school—Grace Dodge Vocational High School—where I was told that I would be a good secretary or cosmetologist. I was enrolled in classes that taught me shorthand and the basics of cosmetology. I was highly unmotivated by the career paths that I was presented with and did not want to become a seamstress, secretary, or cosmetologist. I was not interested in these careers and learning these skills. They were simply not challenging enough and did not capture my imagination, nor did they inspire me. It was only when I enrolled in college that I learned to appreciate the exposure to a typewriter and typing skills.

I became a teenage mom while I was a sophomore in high school and was experiencing a lot of emotional problems and life challenges that most teenagers and my classmates did not have to be concerned about. Although I had the economic support of both parents and a place to live and eat, I experienced life in a way that most adolescents should never have to be exposed to or confronted with.

Me, at age 16, with my newborn baby Monica

I had a child and knew immediately that I wanted a better future for my daughter Monica. I knew that the way out was completing my education and working.

At the end of my high school junior year, my mother and I were called to a meeting with the assistant principal. I was informed that I would have to repeat the eleventh grade. I froze in the chair I was sitting in and did not say much, which was not unusual for me at the time. My mother accepted the decision without much pushback. But I did not want to repeat an entire year just to be miseducated again.

My Baby Monica

I now had a daughter whose future I was consumed with and very concerned about. I wanted so much more for her.

Most of my adolescence I was in shock and numb to the circumstances around me, the exposure to drugs and violence, and the cards that I was being dealt. The discouragement was so great and crushing that I decided on instinct that it was in my best self-interest to sign out of high school and enroll in night school to obtain a GED. I was a teenage mom, and the odds were stacked against me. I did not know it yet, but I had a calling on my life and a destiny to fulfill. Failure was not an option for me, and I could not give up.

I was not aware of the term back then, but I believe that this was when I began learning about not taking no for an answer or allowing others to shape you into who they think you are or what you should be. Some referred to this emerging character trait as being stubborn and rebellious. To a considerable extent, they were correct. What they did not know is that this stubborn and rebellious persistence is precisely what provided me with

I DID NOT KNOW IT YET, BUT I HAD A CALLING ON MY LIFE AND A DESTINY TO FULFILL.

the will and the determination to fight for my self-respect, for my dignity, and for the future of my child. This is where I first started to learn about what it meant to be resilient.

I had a hunger and fire in my soul to rise from the pit of despair that I found myself in. Without any guidance, I figured out that if I attended night school and studied for my GED I would be able to complete my studies with the class of my peers. Six months after enrolling in night school, I passed the GED examination, and I was able to make important decisions about my future. The envelope with my results contained a letter of invitation to enroll at CCNY.

I immediately seized the opportunity. I knew deep inside that this was my golden opportunity to obtain the knowledge and the preparation that I was searching for. This was my shot that would put me on a path of intentionally making change and a difference in the lives of thousands of students. I knew from the moment the door opened for me that I would use my education to become part of the solution. I have continued to share this door of opportunity with all of the "Elaines" who have waited for their shot, and for someone who cared enough to learn about their dreams and to give them a chance to achieve them.

I took odd jobs and worked at places like Chock Full o'Nuts on White Plains Road at the corner of Pelham Parkway, which was the Dunkin Donuts of the 1960s and 1970s. Fortunately, my father would help me with bus fare and an allowance of $5 a week as I was no longer eligible for a school bus pass. The fare was 35 cents each way in 1974. This was what he could afford, and I was grateful. These few dollars would get me through those three months of night school. I would survive on a slice of pizza that was 35 cents and in the mornings one donut that cost 16 cents. A Bodega-bought ham and grilled cheese with coffee or juice all for less than $1 were options as well. Most of the time I just did not eat until I got back home to my mother's delicious home-cooked meals that consisted mostly of Puerto Rican white rice, beans, and fried chicken—my favorite meal.

As a single mom I was eligible for food stamps and aid to dependent children, otherwise known as welfare. In 1974, I applied reluctantly for government assistance. It was not part of our family's experience to ask for help or handouts even when it was necessary. My father was a very proud Puerto Rican man and even in the most difficult of times he refused to apply for welfare benefits. He often worked many hours of overtime well into the late hours of the night, to make ends meet.

As a child I recall the many heated discussions between my mother and father regarding how welfare recipients were viewed and hearing how Papi was too proud to ever have his family go on welfare. A family of four earning an income of less than $3,000 met the poverty line criteria. Although we did not quite meet that, we often went without having enough food to eat. When food was scarce and hard times kicked in Mami would make the best white rice and fried eggs you could ever imagine. This along with the tomato sandwich on white bread was a common part of our diet.

In the 1960s, most working poor families, although not eligible for government assistance and "welfare," were still eligible to receive assistance for food from the Government Surplus program.[16] This program was intended to support the income of farmers who could not sell all of their produce. Almost overnight the farmers began producing as much milk as they could to take advantage of government money. The government purchased the milk dairy farmers

---

16 Erin Blakemore, "How the US ended up with warehouses full of 'Government Cheese,'" August 25, 2023, https://www.history.com/news/government-cheese-dairy-farmers-reagan.

couldn't sell and began to process it into cheese, butter, and dehydrated milk powder.

Families had to meet an income ceiling and apparently ours did. I recall that trucks would drive up to the neighborhood to distribute USDA powdered eggs and milk, peanut butter, blocks of cheese, and canned meat that we now know as SPAM. Hundreds of community residents, including my parents, would stand on long lines to receive the free food supplied by the government. Although only eligible for about two years, this helped to make ends meet. Once we were no longer qualified, we could no longer benefit from the best tasting and saltiest cheese that I ever ate. It is amazing that SPAM has made a comeback and is very popular among college students.

CHAPTER 3

CITY COLLEGE OF NEW YORK: A WORLD OF PURPOSE

"I am not throwing away my shot."
—LIN-MANUEL MIRANDA, *HAMILTON*

I accepted the offer to attend CCNY and was very fortunate to be admitted as a result of student protests to create a more ethnically and racially diverse student enrollment. I was admitted to the SEEK program, under the Open Admissions period in 1975. I must have had an angel on my shoulder, and I was not going to throw away my shot. This phrase, made famous by Lin-Manuel Miranda's Broadway hit *Hamilton*, has a lot of meaning to so many. For me it means not taking life's "no" for an answer. In front of my office, I have intentionally placed a sign that reads "*You will miss the shots that you do not take, 100% of the time.*"

The opportunity to attend college would change the trajectory of my life. The decision that I made to drop out of high school in 1974 and attend night school would put me on a path of making change and a difference in the lives of my own daughter, the personal economy of my family, and thousands of students whom I had not yet met. From the moment that the door opened for me, I was excited and passionate about how I would use my education to become part of the solution. I knew at a very young age that a good solid education was the great equalizer and a critical part of the solution to poverty, hunger, and despair that I witnessed in our neighborhoods.

Enrolling in college would launch my journey toward the completion of a bachelor's degree from CCNY in 1980 in Bilingual Elementary Education. This solid preparation and my great motivation gave me the chance to begin work as a teacher of Puerto Rican and Black children living in poverty in the poorest congressional district in the United States—a community that had the highest infant mortality rate, the highest incidences of drug abuse that was plagued by hopelessness.

In the late 1970s and early 1980s in the aftermath of arson and destruction, parts of the Bronx looked like a war zone. The South Bronx would become a national agenda item for the White House, and presidents of the United States, Jimmy Carter and Ronald Reagan, would visit the aftermath of the arson and make national headlines, delivering speeches on top of the rubble from buildings that were once home to thousands of families. There were many unkept promises to rebuild and restore housing for the hundreds of thousands displaced over the course of a decade. The commitment to invest federal dollars to rebuild the South Bronx would not become a reality for another fifteen to twenty years. It did not appear that poor and working-class Puerto Rican and African American lives mattered.

CITY COLLEGE OF NEW YORK 1975–1980

The neo-Gothic architecture was awe-inspiring and reminded me of the books I had read with stories set in medieval times. When I first stepped onto the campus at CCNY, I was transported to a world that was in stark contrast to the reality of life I lived in the Bronx and the Harlem neighborhood community where the college was located. CCNY was a vibrant environment where students my age from all ethnic and socioeconomic backgrounds were on a mission.

Students were reading, studying for exams, and engaging in conversations about the Civil Rights Movement and the war in Vietnam. There were also parties, students smoking weed, and social distractions everywhere. There were student government and clubs who were preparing to mount protests for a whole number of causes. I enjoyed being part of the very positive hustle and buzz as I went from one building to the next, finding my way through throngs of students

CCNY Shepard Hall.
Source: Caballero1967, CC BY-SA 4.0
<https://creativecommons.org/licenses/by-sa/4.0>,
via Wikimedia Commons

and corridors to class. There were thirty-six acres of tree-lined land located in the Northern Harlem neighborhood, and I had to somehow get from the south campus to the north campus with only as little as fifteen minutes between the time that one class ended and the other began. On the way to classes on the south campus, I would often stop at the falafel truck as it was the only meal that I could afford. I had to ration the $10–$15 that I had for the week and also keep enough money to pay for bus and train fare to and from school.

After a couple of weeks, I immediately felt a sense of belonging and found my tribe: a community of students who were smart, funny, artistic, bold, rebellious, and most of them coming from working-class multicultural communities, such as mine. We were all motivated with goals and a common purpose to obtain a degree and improve our personal economy and that of our families and neighborhoods.

My sense of self-worth and self-esteem began to return. I felt proud of my accomplishments and was finally able to take a deep breath. I had direction and found my path. I was back on track. The courses in philosophy, child development, psychology, ethnic studies, the foundations of education and teaching reading and writing, and curriculum methods and materials were all among my favorite courses. This was the beginning of a journey and the pursuit of knowledge and academic excellence including postgraduate studies that included two Masters of Education and, years later, a Doctor of Education.

> **MY SENSE OF SELF-WORTH AND SELF-ESTEEM BEGAN TO RETURN. I FELT PROUD OF MY ACCOMPLISHMENTS AND WAS FINALLY ABLE TO TAKE A DEEP BREATH. I HAD DIRECTION AND FOUND MY PATH. I WAS BACK ON TRACK.**

It was only much later when I was in graduate school that I learned about and appreciated CCNY's reputation for its academic excellence and status as a college for the working class. The popular titles ranged from the "Harvard of the Proletariat" or "the poor man's Harvard." Of special significance was the fact that ten alumni in the 1950s were recipients of the Nobel Peace Prize. Some students were like me, children of the immigrant diaspora and working-class parents, and soon to become the first in their family to graduate from college. Many students were white and had jobs and families who could support their financial needs.

I was riding trains and taking buses to return to the Bronx, late at night, after a 9 p.m. class. When I arrived home, I had to get ready for my students the next day, prepare lesson plans and materials, and confront the daily challenges of living paycheck to paycheck, balancing my studies and work, and the added responsibility of never quite being able to feel adequate in the management of single mother-hood and the expectations of my family. I would review my daughter's homework and make a list of all the things that I needed to buy for her with my next paycheck. I was doing the best that I could and moved beyond expectations. I was on my way to turning my life completely around and I could not be stopped. Despite this, I lived with a chronic anxiety that I could never do enough, I could not stay home and be who others wanted me to be.

BILINGUAL PUPIL SERVICES 1977–1980

In my junior year at CCNY, I was recruited by Bilingual Pupil Services (BPS), a citywide training program that was federally funded and targeted the education of Puerto Rican and Latino bilingual students to improve their mathematics, reading, and English skills. The requirements were that I worked full time as a teacher intern while completing the rest of my undergraduate studies. There were placement opportunities in school District 7 located in the South Bronx. I eagerly accepted the assignment. I was assigned to Lucila Rodriguez who became my field supervisor for the next two years. I was fascinated by the fact that she shared my mother's name.

CHAPTER 4

THE BRONX IS BURNING: RISING FROM THE ASHES

"Ladies and gentlemen, the Bronx is burning."
—HOWARD COSELL, 1977

When I graduated with my bachelor's degree in education, I wanted to go back to my neighborhood to make a difference and become part of the solution. Upon completion of my experience with BPS, I would later decide to return to the neighborhood to apply to the then New York City Board of Education to work full time as a teacher of children who looked like me and my siblings. In fact, they were me. At twenty-one years of age, I was right back in the South Bronx where my happiest childhood memories, greatest lessons, fears, and disappointments about life were experienced, and the start of my awareness of what systemic racism and educational inequality looked like. Like me, the children needed Puerto Rican educators who cared about their future and were willing to fight for equality in education, and to be part of the solution to change the communities that our people lived in.

On October 12, 1977, during Game 2 of the World Series, the famous sports announcer Howard Cosell announced from the Yankee Stadium "*Ladies and gentlemen, the Bronx is Burning.*" However, the Bronx was burning for nearly a decade preceding this announcement from Yankee Stadium. I was on my way home from CCNY in the Hamilton Heights section of Manhattan on a train heading north on the #4 line into the Bronx. I had to take courses in the evening as I taught until 3 p.m. every day. The trip back home was always an ordeal and survival of the fittest. The trains were overcrowded, dirty, and pickpockets were on the prowl. At least four nights per week, I would board the #1 Broadway at the West 133rd and Amsterdam Avenue to street station to 125th Street to transfer to the #2 West Farms line train to 149th Street to then switch to the #4 Woodlawn line to the Kingsbridge stop and walk over to 196th and the Grand Concourse where my parents lived, and my daughter was being cared for. I would stop there to have a meal and check in on the family. When I switched trains at 149th Street, I could smell fire and as the train approached Yankee Stadium, in the distance I saw a raging fire. This immediately triggered painful memories of our family being burned out of two buildings on Simpson Street. I thought of all the families, the children, and the elderly who would be displaced and prayed, *Lord not again*. As the train got closer the fire seemed to be in my childhood neighborhood. The fire raged for hours.

President Carter visits the site of the Bronx Fires

In 2019, a PBS documentary named the *Decade of Fire* (1968–1978), directed by Vivian Vasquez Irizarry and Gretchen Hildebran, premiered. The documentary chronicles how the unscrupulous and racist landlords torched hundreds of buildings in the South Bronx and the aftermath that resulted in 250,000 human beings who lost their homes. This announcement and the images of buildings burning was televised all over the country and abroad. The directors wove together a unique film that told a very important part of the story for thousands of people who lived in the South Bronx during this period. They documented the horror, the greed, and racism that existed against Puerto Ricans.[17]

When I watched the documentary for the first time, I was transported to those moments of fear and sheer terror as a child living on Simpson Street in the late 1960s and early 1970s. This chapter of my story and the collective experience of a thousand others was finally being told. The exposure of the deliberate arson that was taking place

---

17   Nelson A. Denis, War Against All Puerto Ricans (New York: Nation Books, 2015).

on national television continued to take place after I decided to sign up for a teaching assistant position and return to the South Bronx to start my teaching career. It was 1977, and amid the rubble and despair, I prepared to face my worst fears and to head into the front lines of teaching students in neighborhoods that felt and looked more like a war zone. In fact, the teachers' union argued for combat pay, a bonus afforded to the members of the US armed forces during World War II and serving in dangerous war zones that was not subject to federal taxes.

Photo by Joe Conzo Jr.

Photo by Paula Leon, 1980

The South Bronx was the place where the aromas of the Puerto Rican food cradled my childhood and reminded me of being home with *Mami* and *Papi*. I went back to the neighborhoods where *café bustelo, pan sobao con mantequilla y pastelitos de guava* could be easily found on Westchester Avenue and 156th Street. This was the borough of salsa and where hip hop was born, and where only the strong survived, the home of the Yankees, aka *Bronx Bombers,* and the place where my parents met and made a home in 1954.

> Spanish coffee, soda bread with butter, and guava pastries are all traditional food in a Puerto Rican household served for breakfast or an afternoon treat.

I started my journey as a first-year education associate at twenty-one years of age amid the backdrop of communities suffering from domestic violence, the heroin epidemic, the consequences of poverty, and dangers that lurked in every corner.

EARLY YEARS OF TEACHING (1977–1984)

After graduating from CCNY and completing two years as a Bilingual Educational Associate at Intermediate School (IS) 184 on 778 Forest Avenue, I started employment as a teacher at P.S. 25 on East 149th Street and Tinton Street. When I graduated from CCNY in May of 1980, I was very excited about the placement at another school in the South Bronx. I later learned that the latter placement had a very positive reputation for being the first bilingual/bicultural school in New York City and in the northeastern corridor of the United States.

Hernan La Fontaine, the founding principal of this groundbreaking initiative, had just left to become superintendent of Hartford Public Schools in Connecticut. The school received numerous national recognitions as a school of excellence in bilingual education and the education of native speakers of Spanish. The students are what we now refer to as English Language Learners (ELLs). The school had received federal grants to support bilingual instruction and to serve as a model program for other districts and administrators to follow. During my placement, Luis Cartagena was the principal of P.S. 25 and was recognized as one of the pioneers of bilingual education. He served as principal for over twenty-five years.

CHAPTER 5

NEXT STOP, GRADUATE SCHOOL

> "Blessed with Bilingual Brains"
> **—MARY ASHWORTH**

I graduated college in 1980 with a Bachelor of Science in Elementary Education with a minor in bilingual education. I completed all the education foundation courses, the methods and materials courses, teaching of reading and mathematics, and a specialization in the education of bilingual children. This meant that I was prepared to work with students who were bilingual and bicultural.

Much to my disappointment, my assignment in the fall of 1980 was not as a bilingual teacher, which I knew BPS and the educational courses taken at CCNY sufficiently prepared me for. Instead, the New York City Board of Education office of personnel placed me on an assignment where there were massive shortages for teachers for students with disabilities. I was assigned to work as a special education teacher in a citywide program, responsible to teach fifteen adolescents, fourteen of whom were males, and one female, ranging in age from twelve to fifteen and who had "emotional disturbances." I was advised that this was the only placement available and without any training and preparation for teaching this special population of students. I was directed by the Board of Education at the time to obtain a temporary license for "Teacher of the Emotionally Disturbed." All special education and bilingual programs always seemed to be located on the last floor of the school building. My classroom was on the fourth floor.

On my first days of class, some of the students exhibited moderate to extreme behaviors that were consistent with the low expectations that the NYC public school system had for Black and Brown children. After a short while, it was clear that most were simply lost, depressed, unmotivated, and suffering from years of educational neglect, and teachers who did not care.

My first class of students at PS 25

I was very unprepared to teach this group of high-needs students and was expected to teach without resources and inadequate training. This is where I first learned from the inside how the NYC school system is set up to fail poor students of color and creating conditions for the disparate treatment of students with special needs. I observed students who were predominantly Black and Brown, housed in highly restricted classroom settings that were segregated, and school administrators who had no targets or goals and extraordinarily little expectation for academic progress or improvement in behaviors. The negligence was evident, and it was clear that teachers at the time were just being compensated to show up and manage complex behavior and students who were angry and disengaged. Every effort that I made to teach was met by apathy from the administration as students were not expected to succeed academically. The serious emotional and behavioral challenges that these students exhibited required a comprehensive plan, more resources, curriculum materials, and training for new teachers than what the educational setting provided. There were no textbooks provided, and only a very old black chalkboard and pieces of chalk. It was 1980 and nearly a decade prior to students being given access to technology

My second class of students at IS 139

51

and computers. There were only basal readers and old tattered math and English textbooks that had not been used for years and the students could barely read.

I focused my attention on educating the parents and expressed my concerns to the supervisors of this special education program regarding everything from lack of resources to lack of training and preparation for me as a novice teacher. This is where my awareness of the systemic racism began and what propelled my advocacy for parent and student rights to a quality education. Most of the parents were very grateful for my efforts with their children and made observations about how they never had a teacher who cared about their children. Many of the parents were of Puerto Rican background and Spanish dominant. They would ask to meet with me because they could not speak English and needed assistance with a whole array of services from housing to food stamps applications and appeared to have no place to turn to or simply felt comfortable as I spoke in their language.

Very soon, it became clear that the parents were struggling and needed support above what I could provide. I would refer them to United Bronx Parents (UBP), a community nonprofit that was founded by community leader and activist Dr. Evelina Antonetti. UBP was located on Prospect Avenue and 156th Street, within walking distance of P.S. 25. This was the only resource where I knew that they could find support and assistance. I lasted in this teaching position for one year.

The New York City Board of Education located at sixty-five Court Street in Brooklyn would host an annual hiring hall in the summer, where teachers looking for a position in their borough of residence were in attendance. I was given another assignment in District 7 right in the heart of the most impoverished neighborhood in the South Bronx. In fact, until this day, the area was then and is still now considered the poorest congressional district in the United States and, in fact, poorer than the state of Mississippi. I was placed at IS 139 located at 345 Brook Avenue. IS 139 was in the most dangerous sector of the Bronx that was known for its high crime rate, drug use, domestic violence, and highest infant mortality rate.

I disregarded this reality as my desire and motivation to teach was greater than my fear of the circumstances and the social economic conditions that existed. At this school, I was being given an opportunity to work as a bilingual teacher for a class for students who were learning English as a second language and were also labeled as special education students. To qualify for this assignment, I was provided with a temporary license to teach what was referred to at the time as Bilingual Modified Instructional Services II (MIS) class. I would later have to take a licensing exam for a regular teaching license. It was an exciting new adventure, and I was eager to begin. The school had grades 7–9 with a focus on the arts and music and a federally funded program named the South Bronx Action Theatre.

My third class of students, IS 52

I loved the energy in the neighborhood as it reminded me of home and my parents. It was walking distance to 138th Street, a bustling local shopping district with Puerto Rican-owned bodegas and small food eateries, where I could sit at a counter and buy my lunch that would often consist of *frituras* or a Cuban sandwich, *café latino con la leche herbida*, and *pastelitos de guava* for dessert. Walk a few blocks west and there was the famous Teatro Puerto Rico, an iconic theater that my parents would mention often as the theater that would bring great performances with Puerto Rican actors and singers before I was born. They would proudly boast about the famous artists who traveled from the island to New York City to perform at this theater in the Bronx that belonged to us.

This area of the Bronx with all of its socioeconomic problems was a place where many transplanted Puerto Ricans from the island were able to raise their children and fortunate enough to live in the few tenements that survived the decade of fire, or had apartments in the neighboring housing projects run by the New York City Housing Authority (NYCHA) and, in rare cases, were able to afford to live in the few historic brownstones that lined Alexander Avenue. It was a neighborhood where Puerto Ricans preserved their customs and traditions, spoke their language, listened to salsa music, and were able to be themselves without scrutiny or judgment.

Unfortunately, the neighborhood had a dark side of corruption, high crime rates, violence, drug dealers, and heroin use. Junkies were on every corner and above the fifth-floor landing at rooftops. In the mornings and afternoons, hypodermic needles were scattered everywhere on the ground where children walked to and from school, while police sirens blared. The petty crimes and muggings were rampant; broken windshields and vandalized cars were the norm. My colleagues would provide fair warning that it was a well-known fact that if you had a car and drove it to work, you should not expect to find it in the same condition at the end of the school day. Fortunately, I was a commuter for the first couple of years.

Despite these conditions, I would take the #5 or #2 train from the East Bronx and exit at the Prospect and Westchester Avenue station. I would then walk several blocks to my assignment past the rubble and the dangers that lurked in every corner to meet my class in the schoolyard at 8 a.m. where they would line up to meet their teachers.

My students were predominantly of Puerto Rican descent and first-generation students like me. They all had phenotypes and complexions that were much like me and my siblings. They were Spanish dominant and referred to me as *mee-see* (a Spanish version of Mrs. or Miss). I had fifteen students who were all living in poverty, had limited resources, in need of supervision, and hungry to learn. Some had parents who were struggling to keep their families together or were on drugs or simply were unemployed and could not pay the rent and put food on the table. I immediately fell in love with my students and became very protective of them. After a few weeks of testing me and acting out with a whole array of behaviors, the students' attendance and behaviors improved, and they began to warm up to me and looked forward to coming to school. Once we moved past this pivotal point, I had their attention and could begin to work on classroom structure and prepare them for learning.

I was responsible for teaching remedial reading, English, mathematics, science, and social studies. There was nothing in the room but a black chalkboard and pieces of chalk. I would spend my evenings and weekends working on lesson plans, reviewing textbooks, locating bilingual materials, and preparing projects that would help them to learn. There were so many different ability levels in this one class that I had to keep well-organized and become very creative. The ability levels ranged from nonreaders due to dyslexia to students who were barely reading at a second-grade to third-grade reading level in English or in Spanish. They were in the seventh grade.

My class received so much positive attention on how well-behaved they were. I could not respond to what I learned at that time as the secret ingredient; however, I was reminded of the quote *"No one cares about what you know, until they know how much you care"* by President Theodore Roosevelt. I showed my students how much I cared by consistently preparing well-planned content area lessons that kept them interested, engaged, and on task. I was always present, and incorporated culture and arts into the day for those students who were artistic but could not yet read. For those who were reading between a second- and fourth-grade level, I would search for books that were on their level, and prepared bilingual lessons that would meet the needs for a variety of different learning abilities.

In 1981, I was admitted to a graduate program toward the completion of my first Masters in Bilingual Special Education at Bank Street Graduate School of Education. I was immersed in several theories that included the identification of learning modalities and styles through works by Piaget and Vygotsky. These central theories became the precursor to what influenced my view of intelligence and how students learned. In 1983, the theory of multiple intelligences sparked a new framework for how intelligence was viewed and how teaching methodologies would change. The one size fits all to teaching and learning was challenged when psychologist Dr. Howard Gardner wrote *Frames of Mind: Theory of Multiple Intelligences* (1983).[18] In this book, he launched an exciting and groundbreaking framework that initially included seven intelligences. He argued that all people

---

18   Howard Gardner, Frames of Mind: The Theory of Multiple Intelligences (New York: Basic Books, 1983).

including children possess several intelligences that have implications for how teaching and learning should be designed.

The goal, according to Dr. Gardner, is to tap into the potential of one or more of these seven intelligences. In his 1999 publication *Intelligence Reframed: Multiple Intelligences for the 21st Century,*[19] he added two additional intelligences, for a total of nine, which includes verbal–linguistic, logical–mathematical, musical, body–kinesthetic, visual–spatial, naturalistic, intrapersonal, interpersonal, and existential. This framework created a buzz of controversy and an exciting discourse in the education community throughout the country and revolution around teaching and learning. For teachers, the inherent complexity of this approach was rooted in the preparation and delivery of curriculum and lessons and teaching strategies that would tap into the potential of each of the intelligences. According to Dr. Gardner, it is not a question of whether someone is intelligent, but rather in what way he or she is intelligent. He concludes that each person has a unique profile on how their intelligences are sequenced together. The key is to find the dominant intelligence that will facilitate teaching and improve achievement outcomes for children of color, particularly those with special needs. Two decades after the release of *Intelligence Reframed,* school districts across the country have developed techniques and strategies to apply this theory into practice. This common-sense approach to meeting students where they were on the ability and skills continuum is what I used in my very first classroom in the 1980s, namely, taking students of varying levels of knowledge and skills, and meeting their individual learning needs by preparing lessons according to their intelligence. The application of this methodology

---

19   Howard Gardner, Intelligence Reframed: Multiple Intelligences for the 21st Century (New York: Basic Books, 1999).

gained greater popularity and came to be known as differentiated and scaffolded instruction.[20]

In addition, the work of Russian psychologist Lev Vygotsky (1862–1934) and his *Socio-Cultural Theory of Learning* (1978)[21] had implications for teaching and education. In 1962, he developed the theory of Zone of Proximal Development (ZPD)[22] in response to the Russian system's use of psychometric testing of its children. Central to this theory is the distance between the actual development level and the level of potential development. This theory set the foundation and underpinnings of a new method and approach to teaching and learning that is referred to in the education community as Differentiated Instruction. This method of planning and delivering lessons, for greater achievement outcomes, is today an integral component of effective teaching and lesson planning for any school district that is striving for excellence in student achievement. This is a method consistently implemented at our charter school for the past eighteen years. It is indeed a nonnegotiable practice, and a fundamental resource in the faculty toolbox.

I learned later that the school administration at IS 139 would remark on how I overidentified with my students, and that was not looked upon favorably. This connection and relationship with my students were described as uncommon by many of the white teachers at this school. The display of mutual respect apparently made them feel uncomfortable. They were surprised that I had such great classroom management and how well-structured my class was as they were going

---

20   Pearl Subban, "Differentiated Instruction: A Research Basis," *International Education Journal* 7, no. 7 (2006): 935–947.

21   ev Vygotsky, Mind in Society: The Development of Higher Psychological Processes, ed. Michael Cole, Vera John-Steiner, Sylvia Scribner, and Ellen Souberman (Cambridge, MA: Harvard University Press, 1978).

22   Ibid.

to and from lunch, as well as during morning arrival and afternoon dismissal. Comments such as "you are making us (teachers) all look bad" were ongoing.

I later realized that what they feared was a cultural shift, and that it would soon become obvious that students were being discriminated against and, at times, even mistreated. To be expected to treat students with compassion and respect was too much for them to fathom and they were not ready or willing to step out of their racist mindsets to do so. As a new, young, and idealistic teacher, I clearly did not fit into this culture of low expectations that this administration and the larger school system had for Black and Brown children. I knew that it was just a matter of time before I would be treated with the same level of disregard and disrespect. Without even trying, I became a disruptor to the norm of complacency with student failure, educational negligence, and stereotypes that those in power and influence condoned in the schools at the time. This upheaval was realized simply by teaching students how to read, write, and learn basic mathematics. I introduced history lessons on the lives of civil rights leaders such as Dr. Martin Luther King, Malcolm X, and Harriet Tubman during Black History Month, and taught about Puerto Rican history so that they would learn about their culture and heritage. This was viewed as subversive since Puerto Rican history was not on the school calendar.

Teaching my students became a radical act and yes, they were right, I was more aligned with the experiences of my Black and Brown students and their families. I was more like them, and they were just like me. These students finally had someone who cared enough about them to give them encouragement and hope for the future. I was accused of behaving as if I was better than the white teachers were. Of course, at that time, the concept of cultural competence and socially responsive education was not considered essential when teachers were being interviewed and hired at most NYC public schools. In fact, it is still not a criterion in most school settings today, forty years later. Was this not the point of hiring bilingual teachers who had knowledge of the language, student culture, and an awareness of the social conditions of the neighborhoods where they lived, and the circumstances they woke up to every morning? Was it not to the students' advantage to have a Puerto Rican teacher who understood what it was like to go without food and at times go to sleep hungry, while living in impoverished and frightening conditions?

These early professional memories and my personal experience as a student in the NYC public school system ten years earlier would shape the education leader that I would later become, and helped to inform my education philosophy, core values, and the pursuit of excellence for the benefit of immigrant and first-generation students. These collective experiences contributed to the foundation of my vision for teaching and learning when I decided to start a charter school in the Bronx.

CHAPTER 6

STANDING ON PRINCIPLE IN A RACIALLY HOSTILE ENVIRONMENT

> "We will never stop struggling here in the Bronx
> even though they have destroyed it around us."
> **—DR. EVELINA LOPEZ ANTONETTY**

In the early winter of 1982, I experienced my first major snowstorm as a full-time teacher. On January 13, 1982, 5.8 feet of snow fell on the Bronx. At that time there were no cell phones or internet services to inquire if the school was open and if I should report to work. The school phones at the main office were not being answered, so I simply took the initiative and thought that my students would need me. At IS 139 there were approximately sixty teachers on staff, most of whom lived outside of the city in either upstate New York or in New Jersey. Only a dozen or less of the staff, including me, showed up to work. Although five feet of snow was not considered a major snowstorm and working families in the Bronx still had to report to their places of employment, the schools remained open.

Approximately 90 percent of the teachers did not report to work. In fact, neither did the principal nor his assistant principal. It certainly did not compare to the snowstorm during President's Day week on February 19, 1978, when there was twelve feet of snow that was dumped over the city and shut down businesses and the public schools for an entire week. I recall this time fondly though, as I was working as a paraprofessional at the time and all my teacher friends had a week off and we could simply hang out in each other's homes, play games, eat, and enjoy paid time off. There were abandoned cars and buses that were buried, and the streets were impassable and difficult to walk. It was also a period of freezing weather that fell over the country and NYC. The snow would soon turn into a gray black slush and mountains of dirty snow would line the sidewalks.

However, on this day, students would simply walk to their neighborhood schools. It was the better option since many of the children in the surrounding neighborhood of the South Bronx did not have heat or hot water at home or any food to eat. The schools provided a haven for children living in poverty. As such, the parents sent their children to school since there was heat most of the time, and there were free breakfast and lunch programs that were operating.

I was sent to what seemed to be a music room that had auditorium-style seats. There were approximately fifty students who were being kept there. The school was understaffed and did not have the capacity or the adults present to teach. There were four adults in the room when I walked in, one of whom I later learned was the United Federation of Teachers (UFT) representative. Conflicts ensued between the few students and the teachers who were supervising. It was clear that they were having a lot of difficulty managing this group of students. At some point, shortly after I walked in, a white male teacher cornered an African American adolescent female and started yelling and cursing at her while pointing his finger in her face. The other male that I later learned was his close teacher friend joined in and they ganged up on this Black teenage girl and proceeded to displace all their hate and rage onto her. I was infuriated with what I saw and had to protect the girl from those bigots.

This was the moment where the same white teachers who seemed to be uncomfortable with my idealistic views, and accused me of overidentifying with my students, finally acted out and showed me who they were, who had control of this school, what they thought of me, and my idealistic Puerto Rican ways. The goal was to put me in my place. I simply wanted to be part of the solution and to help. So, I requested that the student be released and given to me so that I could speak with her in hopes of deescalating the situation and quite frankly to protect the student. They both turned on me and yelled, "Mind your business." To that, I responded, "I thought this was my business and why I came into work after a snowstorm and did not stay home like the other teachers did." One of the two teachers who proceeded to escalate the attack against me was the union chapter leader, whose job was to protect the rights of his colleagues and all teachers. Instead, he treated me with the same hatred that he treated the African American student whom he berated. He screamed at me with his finger in my face, "Shut up, we were teaching for years already while you were just learning how to write with your fingers in your own shit!" I was frozen and shocked with fury.

This was clearly intended to put me in my place and to humiliate me. He then pulled me by my arm and practically dragged me to the principal's office. This was my first experience being openly attacked by a crazy white racially biased teacher. He was verbally abusive and treated me as if I was a disobedient child, much in the same way that he was treating the female African American middle school student.

THE FIGHT FOR EQUITY IN THE BRONX

My immediate thought was if this is how he was treating me he must be treating the Black and Brown children far worse. This was clearly his practice and behavior for years, and he was absolutely empowered to do so with no reprimand or interference from others or accountability. He proceeded to make a false complaint about my behavior and how I was interfering with the supervision of the savage and unruly behavior of the handful of students in the auditorium. Apparently, the District 7 Superintendent's office had sent in a "substitute administrator" and district representative to supervise the school. Unfortunately, they did not see, nor hear of what had just transpired and how he was abusing a female student before he then verbally abused me after I intervened to protect a child's interests.

The next day when the school principal did show up, I was called into the principal's office for an investigation. I was brought up on charges and complaints of insubordination by the union representative. The principal was more than happy to support this individual's false allegations. There appeared to be a political arrangement that would benefit him and protect his position. There were many rumors of inappropriate behavior with students, particularly by two teachers who abused the power given by the teachers' union. They controlled the faculty and the principal. It became clear later that he was an alcoholic who would often drink on the job and was using the relationship with the union to protect his position. Any potential exposure of their actions for maintaining a racially hostile environment with unsafe working conditions, which violated the rights of a very outspoken Puerto Rican teacher, was a threat to them. I had no one to turn to at the school, as the very person that should have supported and defended me was the man who attacked me and spewed demeaning racial epithets toward me. This was my introduction to conflict at the workplace and the first impression made by a UFT representative whose behavior was being condoned by an alcoholic and dysfunctional principal. He was being protected in order to remain silent on other abuses that I later learned about, which were being perpetuated by the same teachers who were part of the conflict on that very cold day in January 1982.

I began to channel my outrage at the injustices by seeking out organizations and people who had the same level of indignation and a desire to make changes. My outspokenness and willingness to question authority and speak truth to power over the next decade placed me in a few categories to include a rebellious teacher, a trouble-maker, an angry Puerto Rican woman, and eventually someone to be taken seriously. The negligence and lack of equity fueled my passion and resolve to do more to affect change.

One afternoon the same principal at IS 139 called me into his office to inform me that he would have to give me an unsatisfactory rating for insubordination and that I could be terminated if I did not cooperate with his plan. He wanted me to admit that I was behaving badly on the day of the snowstorm and apologize to the same teachers who attacked me. I stood up for myself and stated that I did nothing wrong and that they were unprofessional and mistreated me. He was clearly being a bully. Why was he not speaking to them this way and why were they not going to be held accountable? With all the

> **THE NEGLIGENCE AND LACK OF EQUITY FUELED MY PASSION AND RESOLVE TO DO MORE TO AFFECT CHANGE.**

righteous indignation that I could muster I stated, *"They should be brought up on charges."* I walked out of his office, and I started walking with great intention toward a public phone booth that was in the lobby. He continued to yell out my name and order me not to walk away. I ignored him and continued walking to the phone booth and closed the door and I knew exactly what to do. I had the number in my hands for UBP and proceeded to call "*Titi*," the mother of the South Bronx, Dr. Evelina Lopez Antonetty, whom I had the privilege of meeting with earlier that school year.

CHAPTER 7

DR. EVELINA LOPEZ ANTONETTY—THE MOTHER OF THE SOUTH BRONX

> "We all have PHDs: Poverty, Hunger and Determination."
> **—DR. EVELINA LOPEZ ANTONETTY**

Dr. Evelina Lopez Antonetty was born in 1922 in Salinas, Puerto Rico. She migrated to the United States in 1933 at eleven years of age and became one of the most respected and revered community leaders, parent and community organizer and educator, and a powerful civil rights activist in New York City. She also became the "mother of the South Bronx" and was lovingly referred to as "*Titi*" (auntie). She was one of my first mentors and from working with her, I learned more about how to fight systems of oppression, educate, and organize parents to fight against a racially biased school system, and how to demand a quality education for our children in our community.

She was the founder and executive director of United Bronx Parents (UBP), established in 1967, which was thirteen years prior to my first meeting with her in 1981 as a very young teacher. The building UBP operated from, located at Prospect Avenue and 156th

Street, was acquired after months of sit-ins and protests led by Dr. Antonetty, who demanded that this abandoned city-owned property be turned over to the organization that she founded for its operations dedicated to providing human services, adult education, free breakfast, and lunch programs as well as parent education to the community.

She was approximately fifty-eight years old at the time that I was introduced to her by a community activist. Evelina was only two years older than my mother. I remember her beautiful smile, kind eyes, and larger-than-life commanding presence. Evelina, as she preferred to be called, moved with great confidence, grace, and an authentic elegance and style that caught my attention. When she spoke with me, I knew that I was in the room with someone whom I could learn from and who cared and understood the frustration, the anger at the injustices in our school system, and the educational neglect that our children had to endure, which would impact the rest of their lives. Evelina understood that our people were suffering, and she actively engaged every willing and committed person to join her in organizing the community and fight for the solutions to the racial and economic disparities that existed.

Dr. Evelina Lopez Antonetty
By Francisco Reyes, 1981, Courtesy the Elba Cabrera Papers, the Archives of the Puerto Rican Diaspora, Center for Puerto Rican Studies, Hunter College, CUNY. - Francisco Reyes, 1981, Courtesy the Elba Cabrera Papers, the Archives of the Puerto Rican Diaspora, Center for Puerto Rican Studies, Hunter College, CUNY., CC BY-SA 4.0, https://commons.wikimedia.org/w/index. php?curid=52080161

After we were introduced, she invited me to sit at a chair in front of her desk. I told her a little bit about myself, and that I was raised in the

South Bronx and recently graduated from college and then she asked me if I was hungry. At that time, I was functioning on adrenaline and would often forget to eat or could not afford to buy more than a $2 lunch. I accepted the meal with a cup of coffee. It felt like home. I informed her that I was a new teacher at IS 139 and wanted to make a difference in the lives of children in the community, and that I was facing roadblocks in doing so. I told her that it did not seem that the principal at my school was interested in a teacher who advocated for her students.

Evelina was very diplomatic but direct, and made it known to me that she had her eye on the schools in District 7 and was aware of the racism and where the problems were. She was quite vocal about the principals and superintendents who were refusing to implement the Aspira Consent Decree[23] and open the bilingual education programs that the districts were receiving funding to run. She was genuine and spoke candidly about her observations and the source of the problems.

While I met with her, there were constant interruptions, a string of continuous incoming calls from congresspeople, elected officials, school superintendents, power brokers, residents, and community activists alike. Her right hand, a community leader and activist named Rosa Escobar, was in and out of the office, reminding her that there were people waiting to see her. The waiting area in the lobby was filled with parents seeking solutions to problems with schools that their children were attending, displaced residents waiting for help with housing applications, government aid, food stamps, or referrals for their loved ones who were addicted to heroin and needed rehabilitation. Those seeking help were the poor and marginalized people

---

23 The 1974 Aspira Consent Decree between the New York City Board of Education and Aspira of New York, established bilingual instruction as a legally enforceable federal entitlement for New York City's non-English-speaking Puerto Rican and Latino students.

with families who were desperate and facing serious quality-of-life problems that needed resolution.

I sat in awe of the energy and the pulse of her office and marveled at how she was able to manage the calls, communicate strategy on what needed to be done for the priorities of the day with a matter-of-fact urgency, while simultaneously making a first-time visitor like me feel welcomed and successfully recruiting a new warrior into her tent. I observed all the interactions, movements, and the tones of the conversations. I looked on with great admiration at Dr. Lopez Antonetty, who to me was someone akin to that of an ambassador of multiple nations. But despite this, she was strategic, fearless, and a great unitarian. She worked with every elected official across party lines and had alliances with individuals who were from diverse religious beliefs and all faiths. Evelina would bring people together who normally would not agree to interact with on their own. She did not entertain petty differences and demanded that everyone come together to solve the problems to child poverty and the education of children, in the poorest congressional district of the country. She would host meetings at her office and each party had to put aside their differences and politics, for the benefit of the greater good and a larger plan and vision. These meetings would take place among politicians, businesspeople, gang leaders, educators, civil rights leaders, priests, Pentecostal church ministers, and leaders from the African American community. The diverse profile and politics of those who sought out Evelina ranged from white liberals to the radical left, religious conservatives to atheists, and Puerto Rican revolutionaries, socialists, nationalists, and communists. They would all schedule time with Evelina and ask for guidance and support with their political campaigns, local neighborhood initiatives, racial and social justice agendas, and global issues. The colonial status of Puerto Rico was a major issue and an important agenda item for Evelina, who was influenced by Dr. Pedro Albizu Campos and the Independence Movement on the island in which thousands of Puerto Ricans[24] were fighting, against colonialism and to win independence from the United States.

It became clear that I was in the company of greatness. Here was a powerful woman who was an advocate, a maternal figure to the community she served, the protector of the civil rights of Puerto Ricans, and devoted to the South Bronx and its people to the very end of her life. Her warmth, commanding presence, and compassion toward others made an impression on me as a young teacher, leader, and budding activist. Evelina was a model of leadership that I have never forgotten, and I have sought to incorporate her practice into my work and relationships with the community that I continue to serve today and throughout the past forty years.

Dr. Evelina Antonetty Mural, South Bronx, 1980
Photo by Joe Conzo Jr., Mural by TatsCru

---

24   Nelson A. Denis, War Against All Puerto Ricans: Revolution and Terror in America's Colony (New York: Nation Books, 2015).

Puerto Rican Nationalist Lolita Lebron (left), and Dr. Evelina Lopez Antonetty (right)
Photo by Joe Conzo Jr.

At the end of my visit, she advised me to let her know if I had any issues or problems with anyone at the school and to contact her if I needed her help. When our meeting ended, I knew that I could trust her and I did contact her when the attacks condoned by the principal inevitably escalated. Evelina coached me to write a letter and request a meeting with Community School District (CSD) 7 Superintendent Carmen Rodriguez to address my concerns, so I did. Not having heard back from the district superintendent, I decided to stage a one-person sit-in at her office for approximately three hours. I was determined not to move from the hard wooden bench in her waiting area until I was seen and heard by Ms. Rodriguez. Surely the superintendent who was also Puerto Rican would be empathetic and interested in being informed of the discriminatory practices and abuses that I had experienced under the administrative authority of the principal. But that was not the case, much to my surprise.

Her deputy superintendent, Harold Levy, came out to the waiting room several times to inform me that Ms. Rodriguez was busy and was not available to meet with me. He advised me that if I did not leave, I would be charged with insubordination. This charge had grave consequences as it meant an unsatisfactory rating, and my license as a new teacher could also be revoked. I was indignant and had committed to my one-woman protest and my very first act of civil disobedience. But instead of a discussion, I found myself being threatened by her deputy superintendent with being fired or arrested, simply for requesting a meeting to protect my human rights.

I felt defeated, as there was too much at stake for me to risk losing my job. My livelihood, all my arduous work for five years to earn my college degree and teaching license while working full time and juggling responsibilities as a single parent at twenty-five years of age. Not to mention the embarrassment and how disappointed my parents would be. I decided to leave and consider what to do next.

My daughter Monica and I in my classroom, 1981

This was my first lesson at accepting defeat in the New York City public school system, as I weighed the benefits of losing the battle to win the war. My youthful idealism and sense of indignation would have to be put on hold, at least temporarily. This experience propelled my anger and furthered my resolve to continue working at the grassroots level, educating my students, and empowering parents on pursuing their rights, asking questions, and fighting until they were heard. I learned how to continue fighting this time with the support of others, using the organizing skills that I was introduced to by Evelina and UBP. At the end of the school year, I was reassigned to another school district, and this ensured that I would not lose my license and would be able to continue teaching. Although this was never confirmed to me directly, I am sure that this outcome was the work of "Titi." She was in close contact with Ms. Rodriguez, who was not pleased with the implications of having a whistleblower ready to expose what was being allowed in a school in her district on her watch. Evelina was aware of my situation and wanted to protect me from more harassment and from losing my job. In the fall of 1983, I was transferred to IS 52 in District 8 on Kelly Street, right across the street from People's Park.

I returned to UBP as a volunteer on a dozen or more occasions over a three-year period, where I learned how to organize the community effectively, using their model for empowering parents on a whole number of issues that needed to be changed in the school system. I had a front row seat and was able to witness how Evelina engaged in battle against the rampant discrimination against Puerto Rican children, as well as the dismantling of bilingual education programs.

I had the privilege of accompanying her with members of UBP and the NCPRR[25] to attend a school board meeting at P.S. 130 that was located at 750 Prospect Avenue right across the street from UBP. Max Messer presided as the CSD superintendent for District 8. He was disrespectful and dismissive when it was Evelina's turn to speak to the board. He looked up at the ceiling the entire time and refused to give her eye contact or the respect that she merited. She accused Mr. Messer who was leading this district in the South Bronx at the time as being a racist. His face turned beet red in anger and the parents and the community cheered her on. The school board chair hit her gavel on the table calling for order in the room.

> The National Congress for Puerto Rican Rights (NCPRR) was created in 1981 by a diverse group of Puerto Rican activists from many different existing organizations such as the Young Lords, the Puerto Rican Socialist Party (PSP), and the Puerto Rican Alliance (PRA). Former members of the Young Lords like Juan Ramos (from Philadelphia) and Juan Gonzalez, Hilda Mar Ortiz and Richie Perez (from New York) wanted to create a larger civil rights organization which could mobilize Puerto Rican communities across the nation on a variety of issues.

The parents and activists were fired up and ready to continue the fight. They took their turns one by one to speak about their opposition to his discriminatory policies. This board meeting was my first lesson in the confrontation of authority and speaking truth to power.

---

25 Ariel Arnau, "Suing for Spanish: Puerto Ricans, Bilingual Voting, and Legal Activism in the 1970s" (The Graduate Center, City University of New York, 2018).

It was not until 1997 that Mr. Messer resigned under pressure from the group known as Mothers on the Move (MOM).[26] During Messer's twenty-one years at the top administrative level of the district, MOM charged that schools in the poorer areas had been ignored while those in the wealthier parts had enjoyed generous funding, and were thereby able to achieve better test scores, as well as receive more attention and greater instructional interventions for their children.[27] MOM members had railed against the inequity in angry letters and impassioned pleas to the school board and elected officials.

26   Jason Tanz, "Not your mother's PTA," https://www.edweek.org/education/ not-your-mothers-pta/2001/02.

27   Maria Alvarez, "Some tough mothers – the wisdom of Wanda Salaman – motivating moms to save our schools," https://nypost.com/2005/05/11/some-tough-mothers-the-wisdom-of-wanda-salaman-motivating-moms-to-save-our-schools/.

CHAPTER 8

THE IVY LEAGUE STUDENT AND SOCIAL ACTIVISM

> "Education is the most powerful weapon
> which you can use to change the world."
> **—NELSON MANDELA**

I n 1984, after completing my first master's degree at Bank Street College on the Upper West Side of Manhattan, I decided that it was not enough to earn only a master's degree, so I chose to pursue postgraduate studies toward a doctorate. Over a period of seven years, I commuted each day on the #1 Broadway line first to and from CCNY at 138th Street and then later to Bank Street College on West 112th Street, where the train would pass the 116th Street stop for Columbia University. I was very curious about this campus and would frequently imagine myself proudly walking onto those green, perfectly manicured lawns, with beautiful architecture that was a sharp contrast to the Gothic architecture of the buildings at CCNY, which had been the style of great American universities at the time.[28] This style was often seen in institutions of higher learning,

---

28 Columbia College Today, https://www.college.columbia.edu/cct_archive/jan02/jan02_cover_architecture.html.

because during the nineteenth century the architects and benefactors had supported an adoption of classicism for its buildings.

As an undergraduate student, I had no idea what the substantive difference was between a public and private institution of higher education. All I knew was that it was beyond my reach financially, with very expensive tuition and unrealistic for a single mom. This was before the internet, when I could not conduct my own research to find out what programs and financial aid were available to me. Unbelievably, there was no information available at the financial aid office or at the admissions office. The possibility of scholarships was not provided or discussed by my advisers or faculty members while I was an undergraduate. I only learned about scholarships to assist with tuition while studying at Bank Street College. TC at Columbia University was my dream school and next stop.

The term "Ivy League" had been coined by sportswriter Caswell[29] as a reference to the powerful eastern football league, from the eight universities of Harvard, Princeton, Yale, Penn, Dartmouth, Cornell, Columbia, and Brown. Of all the institutions of higher learning, these elite schools are the most outstanding and the most sought-after in terms of acceptance and graduation. Over a third of US presidents attended an Ivy League school, and collectively they have an impressive share of Nobel laureates.[30] But always on the lookout for possibilities, I listened to the conversations among my classmates and learned that TC at Columbia University was often the next high aspiration for graduates who were in serious pursuit of a doctorate in education, and especially for those aspiring to become curriculum experts, principals, and district superintendents.

29   Jessica Spradling, "Origins of the term 'Ivy League' remain mysterious," 2003, https://badgerherald.com/news/2003/03/03/origins-of-the-term/.

30   U.S. News Staff, "Ivy league schools," https://www.usnews.com/education/best-colleges/ivy-league-schools.

I also learned while conducting research that less than 2 percent of Puerto Rican/Latino professionals were enrolled and graduated. At the time there were federal incentives such as Title VII, where students pursuing a minor in bilingual education could apply to TC and obtain 50 percent of the tuition paid. Of course, this meant that a federal student loan would be necessary to pay the balance of the tuition not paid by the grant. I excelled as a graduate student at Bank Street College, and I had developed enough confidence by then to believe there was nothing that I could not achieve or conquer. When I started the application process, the office of admission at TC advised me that I could have all forty-five of my graduate credits that were higher than a B transferred for review and consideration. This would essentially cut down the ninety-credit requirement to qualify for a doctorate with the forty-five credits earned with my masters. In the spring of 1984, I received a letter from the Office of Admissions that my application was accepted, and that all the credits I had earned at Bank Street College were eligible for transfer.

I was overjoyed and at the same time in disbelief that just ten years earlier, I was a high school "pushout"[31] from the South Bronx who would now be admitted into an Ivy League school! It only made sense that I would aim higher and apply there. My goal was to obtain the highest credentials possible so that I could be prepared to meet and leverage every opportunity that presented itself, with a vision to create something great for the young people in the community which would address issues of equity in education and open the doors to college. During this time I was actively engaged in social activism and educational advocacy defending the rights of Puerto Rican children to a quality education and the preservation of bilingual education programs.

---

31   Monica Ruth Rouse, "Pull and Push Factors That Influence a Student's Decision to Drop Out of School," (*Walden Dissertations and Doctoral Studies*, 2019), 7071.

I volunteered a great deal and helped to organize many of the local forums to fight for the rights of our children to receive these programs.

I was twenty-nine years of age during my first year at TC. It was quite an adjustment, as it was a world apart from my reality and life's circumstances. My classmates were predominantly white, born and raised in upper-middle-class families. Many of my classmates did not have to work for a living, nor be concerned about financial aid and how the balance of their tuition would be paid. Most students were liberal in their politics and wanted to do good and "save" poor children of color from the socioeconomic conditions. Those with the *"savior syndrome"* appeared to feel guilty that they were so privileged while many children were stuck in poverty-stricken neighborhoods.

During this period in the 1980s, there was a war on poverty that was launched at a national level. The US Secretary of Education, Terrence Bell, appointed by President Ronald Reagan, released a national report titled *A Nation at Risk*.[32] The Reagan administration created a commission to study the crisis in American education. There were nationwide concerns about the demise of the academic rigor of the past, and that American schools were being outperformed by other countries throughout the globe. According to National Public Radio (NPR), *A Nation at Risk* cited statistics such as: "The average achievement of high school students on most standardized tests is now lower than twenty-six years ago when Sputnik was launched" and "[The SAT demonstrates] a virtually unbroken decline from 1963 to 1980. Average verbal scores fell over 50 points and average mathematics scores dropped nearly 40 points."

This put education at the front and center of national politics and gave way for the No Child Left Behind Act. Some of my peers

---

32   Jennifer Park, "A nation at risk," 2004, https://www.edweek.org/
      policy-politics/a-nation-at-risk/2004/09.

appeared to feel uncomfortable when I spoke up in class to question or challenge the ideas being presented, the philosophies behind the concept, and conclusions that were being presented to a class full of very eager and wide-eyed graduate students. There was tension at the convergence of ideas and discourse, which conflicted with my practical experience and ideals about teaching Black and Latino children.

In most of my postgraduate courses, I was the only woman of color in the room with "*street credit*" and an intimate understanding of the neighborhoods where the students that they encountered lived. There was a whole array of topics regarding the education, progress, and achievement potential of Black and Latino students, and I believed that I understood this completely through first hand experience. I vividly recalled my challenges as a Puerto Rican child in the NYC public school system. My professors at TC were speaking about students who fit my profile as an elementary and junior high school student, and very similar to the experiences of the students that I had taught. I listened with intention and was highly critical of many of the precepts being presented when it came to children who were raised in similar circumstances.

Although not a popular construct at the time, I was able to identify the lack of social responsiveness, cultural incompetence, and disconnection to the world that students of color lived in. Most of my classmates were white and raised in privilege, had never taught in the South Bronx, nor had ever stepped foot in any of the poor embattled neighborhoods such as Harlem, Bedford Stuyvesant, Bushwick, or Red Hook. Their placements were in private schools where children were white and middle class. They commuted from various states in the northeastern corridor or lived in the Upper West Side. I was riding trains late at night to return home to the Bronx. I was an intelligent and determined Puerto Rican woman who had found her confidence and voice. I became outspoken and was often very passionate and ready to assert my differences with the ideas being presented.

When classes resumed, I had an opportunity in my dissertation seminars to share some of these ideas, and it was very disappointing and often discouraging to hear some of those who were enrolled in the same dissertation seminar with me having such low expectations for children of color. Both Latino and white colleagues would challenge me on my ideas and were very vocal in expressing that what I was proposing was not possible. My ideas were highly scrutinized by a few of my peers and criticized for being idealistic and not in touch with the reality of students living in poverty. It appeared that proposing an institution with high expectations and an academically rigorous curriculum for students in the Bronx was not a very popular construct and took the educators in the room out of their comfort zone. After all, what I was proposing was unheard of in any school in the Bronx and this would threaten the status quo.

My audience included a body of my peers and educators who were former NYC Board of Education teachers who had moved up to administrative positions working in the archaic and racially entrenched NYC Board of Education, which has historically perpetuated a system of discrimination and failure of Latino students for decades. By 1990, the consequences of tracking and poor education contributed to more than 70 percent of Latino students dropping out of high school,[33] which created an underclass of marginalized young people who for decades later were only eligible for menial jobs. These were the victims of systemic racism. They would become the targets and fertile ground for the school-to-prison pipeline.[34]

---

33   Lucy Hood, *High School Students at Risk: The Challenge of Dropouts and Pushouts* (New York: Carnegie Corporation of New York, 2004).

34   Monica Ruth Rouse, "Pull and Push Factors That Influence a Student's Decision to Drop Out of School."

Like me, many of my classmates were aspiring to earn doctorates and earn positions as education administrators, assistant principals, principals, or superintendents. When I got to the part where all students would be treated the same, and how learning would be accelerated with access to the same material, I received no encouragement and did not feel supported at all. I made a passionate presentation that if all students were treated as inherently gifted and talented it was possible. However, it was concluded that these were all very unrealistic and ambitious ideas. I was not deterred, and this further fueled my convictions that all students could have equal access to the keys to the "*Kingdom of Knowledge*" and experience learning in a setting that would aim toward excellence and open a path to higher education. My goal would be not only to provide a high-quality education—I was committed to changing the future of our youth and to impact their personal economy. They would in turn be empowered and provided with the tools to change the lives of their communities. Why couldn't our students be programmed for Yale instead of jail? This is what social justice and equity in education for students of color living in poverty and marginalized by the system looked like to me.[35]

On my way to my doctorate, I earned my Ed.N, a second masters in education administration at TC, 1989.

---

35   Sofia Bahena, *Disrupting the School-to-Prison Pipeline* (Cambridge: Harvard Educational Review, 2012).

CHAPTER 9

EARNING THE DOCTORATE— WALKING THROUGH THE GAUNTLET

"Failure is not an option."
—GENE KRANZ

I decided not to work full time and instead took on consultant and adjunct work teaching graduate courses in the Bilingual and Special Education and the Politics of Education at a few CUNY schools and at Bank Street College. It was a financial strain, but I needed to finish my doctoral degree.

While working on my degree, on long weekends I would sometimes take a break and drive out to either the tip of Long Island to Montauk or Cape Cod, which were my favorite seaside towns in the northeast coast. I absolutely loved the freedom that I experienced walking alongside the ocean, hearing the waves crashing, and watching the birds flying overhead. The water has always had a calming effect on me. On this trip, I was searching, although I was not sure for what. I knew I needed to be alone. I was experiencing so many personal and emotional challenges that were burdening my soul, and I needed to get away and clear my head. So, I planned a whale-watching trip out of Provincetown.

This was an amazing experience that came at exactly the right time in my journey. When you are on a ferry in the middle of the ocean and you experience a whale launching itself out of the water for the very first time, it is breathtaking and puts your place in the world into perspective. I felt so small when compared with the vastness of the ocean, and although I was a bit seasick, the miracle of seeing not one but four whales was an impactful spiritual moment in my life.

I headed back to New York in a flood of traffic. What I thought would be a five-hour trip easily turned into a nine-hour odyssey back home to the Bronx. I was exhausted. But as I drove back on the highway, I had plenty of time to think and to reflect on what I wanted to do with my life after the doctorate and where I wanted to take this amazing opportunity that I had been given.

I had for a very long time been a passionate education advocate and social justice activist regarding issues of equity in education for the migrant and immigrant Latino students, particularly those who were ELLs. While I continued the long drive home from Cape Cod to the Bronx, I began to craft a plan to start a school and what the mission, goals, teaching, learning, and curriculum would look like. In my mind I reviewed the design of all the components of this vision that was placed into my heart and mind. I didn't know where I should start, whom to approach, or how to begin.

When I returned to my home office, at the first opportunity I started drafting an outline to write a proposal for my concept that fourteen years later would serve as the seeds for what is today the International Leadership Charter High School. My personal educational philosophy and the type of school that I wanted to create was still in development. I wasn't sure if it was going to be a private independent school or a public school. All I knew was that the school that I visualized had students who would not be labeled or stigmatized, and who would be given an equal opportunity to work with the same rigorous academic content and exposure to all the knowledge, materials, resources, and experiences that white children of privilege have historically received.

This vision sustained me during those nine years of extremely intense and rigorous postgraduate coursework. After the doctoral certification and three years of writing, I finally completed a dissertation manuscript that was ready to be professionally bound and ready for defense. At least that was what I believed to be the case. The process was one hurdle after another, and some of those hurdles included highly regarded tenured professors who were the gatekeepers to the coveted doctoral degree. I was at their mercy: only they could legitimize the process and agree that I was ready and allow me to pass through the "veil."

As a doctoral candidate, I could select and invite the professors within the department as advisers and members of my dissertation committee. They would serve as the panel of experts in reading the chapters, provide feedback to improve the writing on their own timeline, and interject ideas for inclusion, whether I felt they were related to the hypothesis that I was seeking to prove or not. These advisers would have the power to tear my work to pieces and delay the process for another four years. I likened the process to selecting your own executioner.

Throughout those three years of the program, I was in an All but Dissertation (ABD)—a designation given by institutions after all your coursework and certification exams have been completed. I was a certified doctoral student and had to maintain an enrollment status for a hefty registration fee of approximately $5,000 per semester. Doctoral students at the ABD stage are paying simply to maintain good academic standing at the university, a requirement to avoid being dropped from the doctoral program.

For my dissertation committee, I selected Dr. María Torres-Guzmán, who at the time was the department chair of the Bilingual/Bicultural department at TC. This was a course of study that I was very passionate about and one that many of my colleagues minored in. Professor Emerita María Torres-Guzmán was a pioneer in the field

of multilingual and multicultural education. Sadly, she passed away in 2018 in Madrid, Spain. María's life was about fighting for social justice through the Bilingual/Bicultural Education department. Part of her legacy at TC was to defend and promote linguistically minoritized groups' languages, cultures, and identities, and she saw bilingual education as an important educational vehicle to support the learning of children from these groups. Dr. Torres-Guzmán was an accomplished researcher and author of several publications. She was a fierce

Dr. María Torres-Guzmán and I, joined by professors from the Bilingual/Bicultural Department at TC

advocate for her program and her students. She was "the face and the heart of the bilingual education program at TC, and always will be," said A. Lin Goodwin, TC Vice Dean and Professor of Education.

Her numerous publications include *Learning in 2 Worlds: An Integrated Spanish/English Biliteracy Approach*[36] and *Freedom at Work: Language, Professional and Intellectual Development in Schools.* Torres-Guzmán and coauthor Ruth Swinney chronicle the transformation of P.S. 165, and a landmark edited volume stemming from a national conference titled *Imagining Multilingual Schools: Languages in Education and Globalization* (Multilingual Matters 2006).

According to María, "We can talk about standardization and accountability as a way of achieving equity, but we have ample evidence that the freedoms within the curriculum, what is taught and what is measured, are curtailed and the outcomes are greater gaps."

In addition, I selected Dr. Dennis Mithaug who was the Department Chair of the Special Education Department. Professor Mithaug and his colleagues also developed a theory of learning that placed self-engagement at the center of why, how, and what people learn whether they are disabled or not. He was a founding member and president of the Division for Research at the Council for

> **"WE CAN TALK ABOUT STANDARDIZATION AND ACCOUNTABILITY AS A WAY OF ACHIEVING EQUITY, BUT WE HAVE AMPLE EVIDENCE THAT THE FREEDOMS WITHIN THE CURRICULUM, WHAT IS TAUGHT AND WHAT IS MEASURED, ARE CURTAILED AND THE OUTCOMES ARE GREATER GAPS."**
>
> **—DR. MARÍA TORRES-GUZMÁN**

---

36   Bertha Perez and Maria Torres-Guzman, *Learning in 2 Worlds: An Integrated Spanish/ English Biliteracy Approach* (English and Spanish Edition, 1994).

Exceptional Children—facts that I learned after selecting him to serve on my committee. His credentials put into perspective his relentlessly tough approach to the data that I presented as part of the quantitative research study for my dissertation.[37]

I frequently expressed my concerns throughout this grueling process and was reassured by Dr. Torres-Guzmán that rarely, if ever, would a doctoral candidate fail by the committee at a dissertation defense. It was explained that once you were assigned your dissertation defense date, the committee had predetermined that you were ready. Also, your adviser would not allow you to proceed to your defense unless she was confident you would succeed. If you didn't succeed, she would look bad in front of her colleagues. All I had to do was show up, remain calm, focus on responding to the questions, and under no circumstance present or say something inappropriate, completely outrageous, or off-topic.

For many, the dissertation defense experience is a daunting rite of passage, a walk through the gauntlet. For me, this remained true as described by others in the same cohort and created a great deal of anxiety. Not surprisingly, the night before I had to appear for the actual defense in April of 1994, I had nightmares. In my dreams I found myself in one of the rooms within TC where the dissertation defense would take place. I saw my dissertation had been shredded to pieces. This was followed by a subsequent nightmare when I arrived in the classroom where the dissertation defense was taking place, and all my advisers on the committee had left because I did not arrive on time.

---

37 Elaine Ruíz-Rodriguez, "Language Attitudes of Teachers: Its Relationship to the Referral of the Linguistically and Culturally Diverse Student to Special Education" (PhD diss., Teachers College, Columbia University, 1994), ProQuest Dissertations Publishing.

This nightmare turned into a blessing since arriving to places ahead of time had always been a struggle for me. The morning of my defense, I made a point of getting up very early and called a cab so that I did not have to waste time trying to find parking. I arrived at the assigned room at Grace Dodge Hall before the dissertation committee did. I had a nervous flutter in the pit of my stomach and felt sick to my stomach. Despite this, I looked good, in my carefully selected professional wardrobe, with dissertation in hand, and was ready to go into the "defense" mode. No one had arrived yet, and I anxiously waited for ten minutes, though that seemed like an eternity to me.

The thought crossed my mind that I may have had the wrong day, location, or room number. I recalled the dream that I had the previous evening, and it further triggered my anxiety. Then suddenly the door opened, and it was Professor Mithaug who was the first to greet me. He extended his hand, and as he smiled at me, he said "Congratulations!" But I could not fully celebrate this moment at that point because I knew I had not gone through the defense yet. I took this kind gesture as a signal from him that I should relax, and that I was going to do well in the defense of my dissertation.

The previous three years of writing, requests for edits, revisions and rewriting all the chapters submitted was one of the greatest tests in academic scholarship and endurance that I had ever experienced as a postgraduate student. I knew that I couldn't give up, and of course there were many tears, sleepless nights, and at some points anger and frustration toward members of my committee. Even though this all paid off in the end, I would provide them with chapters of my dissertation, and they would not get back to me or provide me with any feedback for weeks and at times even months. I had to frequently assert myself, visit their offices and make calls, leave notes and messages, and gently inquire if they had read the most recent submission of my revised chapters. I was consistently given back chapters that clearly had not really been thoroughly or thoughtfully read, with scribbled comments that I could not use or intelligently decipher, as they required clarification and interpretation. I approached the chair of my defense committee, Dr. Torres-Guzmán, who did indeed provide a lot of comments, many of which were very helpful but even in that case, I found myself editing the chapters back to the way they were at the beginning when I first submitted them. It was a very frustrating part of the process that felt like torture.

I was told very directly that all doctoral students, including my professors, had to go through similar rigor, pain, and frustration on the way to earning a terminal degree. All who were expecting to receive a doctorate from an Ivy League institution had to do so by submitting themselves to this intentionally grueling process and endure the informal walk through the gauntlet to earn the privilege of joining the less than 2 percent Latina women in the country who hold a doctoral degree.[38] As a Puerto Rican woman of color raised in the South Bronx who could no longer afford to pay an annual enrollment fee on an educator's salary, to remain in good standing, I had to question the protracted process and what appeared at times to be the over-scrutiny of my work. This did not sit well with me because I was not working full time and was having a lot of personal and financial challenges. It was probably the very first time that I was terribly afraid of failing since 1975, when I first enrolled at CCNY as an undergraduate student. Failing was not an option. There was a lot at stake.

On May 9, 1994, I finally graduated with a doctoral degree in education. There were two ceremonies that took place. The first was

38 Stafford Hood and Donald Freeman, "Where Do Students of Color Earn Doctorates in Education? The "Top 25" Colleges and Schools of Education," *The Journal of Negro Education* 64, no. 4: 423–436. https://doi.org/10.2307/2967265.

THE FIGHT FOR EQUITY IN THE BRONX

with the entire Columbia University graduating class of 1994, with all the various schools represented to include the schools of law, engineering, medicine, political science, and education. The second ceremony took place at Riverside Church on the same day. It was quite an exhausting but beautiful moment. My parents, Lucila and Alfonso Sr., my younger brother, Alfonso Jr., my daughter Monica, and my fourteen-month-old granddaughter Miraya Alexis were all in attendance. As I walked up to the seats where the class of 1994 graduates were seated at Columbia University's great lawn, the sun was beaming and there was a positive hum of chatter and exuberance in the air. Besides my daughter's birth, her graduation from high school (and since, my marriage to Tony in 2001), it was one of the happiest days and greatest moments of my life. My thoughts were that now I had a chance to fulfill the vision that I had that weekend while I spent the day alone at Cape Cod.

CHAPTER 10

EDUCATION AS A CIVIL RIGHT: A VISION FOR EQUITY IN THE BRONX

> "If we [are] already bilingual," she asked, "why should our children lose their language and only speak one language, English?"
> **—DR. ANTONIA PANTOJA**

For nearly a decade, while simultaneously pursuing my postgraduate degrees at Bank Street College and TC at Columbia University, I was very active in social justice causes and became a member and leader in NCPRR NYC Chapter from 1981 to 1995[39] and worked in coalition with other civil rights organizations, meeting a cadre of like-minded individuals locally and nationally. NCPRR was founded by former leaders of the YLP in 1981 in the South Bronx. Fresh out of college, I was recruited by Dr. Diana Caballero, founding member of NCPRR, who shared a panel with me at CCNY. I agreed to join her and other education and community activists, and was invited to participate

---

39 The Committee Against Fort Apache Protesting Media Stereotypes, https://phi. history.cornell.edu/projects/archival-finds/the-committee-against-fort-apache/.

in various protests, as well as multilingual coalition meetings with various community advocacy organizations. This is where I learned the most important lessons in community organizing, strategy, and speaking boldly against racism and inequity.

The NCPRR was created in 1981 by a diverse group of Puerto Rican activists from many different existing organizations such as the Young Lords, the Puerto Rican Socialist Party (PSP), and the Puerto Rican Alliance (PRA). While early meetings took place in Philadelphia, its first large convention was in the Bronx. Former members of the Young Lords like Juan Ramos (from Philadelphia) and Juan Gonzalez, Hildamar Ortiz, and Richie Perez (from New York) wanted to create a larger civil rights organization that could mobilize Puerto Rican communities across the nation on a variety of issues. The structure of the organization was designed to be decentralized; while the NCPRR did have a central executive committee, much of its organizing energy came from local branches throughout the northeastern part of the United States. New York City was among its strongest chapters.

This became a vehicle where I was able to channel my outrage at the injustices that I continued to witness and experience as a young teacher. Eventually I was completely consumed with this critical aspect of advocacy at a volunteer level and became a community leader defending the language rights of children and later in the 1990s opposing the "English-Only" movement[40] fueled by anti-immigrant sentiments and xenophobia at a local and national level.

I was asked to speak at hearings and to support parent groups at parent association and school board meetings. I spoke on their behalf and in defense of the rights of Puerto Rican and Latino children to a bilingual education and programs that would provide greater equal educational opportunities than what they were receiving. I traveled late into the night to and from meetings throughout the city—from the Bronx to Queens and often to school districts in Suffolk County, participating in public hearings where I provided testimony. I immersed myself in the reading of cases that had been fought and won in the federal and local judicial system that would mandate the US Department of Education (DOE) to create policies and regulations that would force public school districts into compliance. The timing of the required study of legislation and education law that guided policy in New York and the country was serendipitous. Without question, the graduate courses at TC provided me with an intellectual context, the legal underpinnings, as well as the historical precedence of the roots of educational policy geared toward protecting the rights of language minority students in the public schools in New York and the entire country.

The incongruence of what was written in the laws, and the lack of implementation of the regulations guided by policy, could not be reconciled by me and other activists who witnessed events, read reports, and heard testimonies from parents and teachers of how these policies were being continually broken and violated in New York City public schools. The greatest impact was on the education of immigrant and non-immigrant children who were native speakers of languages other

---

40   Ariel Arnau, "Suing for Spanish: Puerto Ricans, bilingual voting, and legal activism in the 1970s."

than English and were being raised in a multicultural context and legally entitled to bilingual education programs.

Historically, this population of students was being blatantly denied these programs throughout the late 1970s. With a new wave of awareness and pressure from legal advocacy groups and community organizations, there was a greater attention being paid to the compliance with these programs during the 1980s and 1990s. It was far worse for special education students who were bilingual and bicultural. In very large numbers, these students were being erroneously labeled, misplaced, and overrepresented in classes for the speech and language impaired or the emotionally disturbed.

For Latino students, who were eligible for bilingual instructional services under the law, these programs were essential and a foundation of their academic achievement. I would write letters on behalf of parents and members of the community and boldly demand of superintendents, principals, and school districts the full implementation of the program that children were entitled to, in accordance with the state and local laws and regulations, namely the Aspira Consent Decree of 1972,[41] a landmark case that was argued in the context of established desegregation laws that outlawed "separate but equal "schooling in the United States (Brown v. Board of Education 1954; the Civil Rights Act of 1964) and the fight for community control in the 1960s and 1970s. Many Puerto Rican leaders, parents, attorneys, and educators argued that the city's schools were obligated to provide instruction that addressed their linguistic and cultural needs. Ultimately the case was litigated and won by the Puerto Rican Legal Defense fund and the courts ruled in favor of the plaintiffs, finding

---

41 Anthony De Jesús and Madeline Perez, "From Community Control to Consent Decree: Puerto Ricans Organizing for Education and Language Rights 1960s and '70s New York City," *Centro Journal* 21, no. 2: 7–31.

that children who were not dominant in the English language had the right to instruction in their native language.

In response to high dropout rates and the steady disenfranchisement of Puerto Rican students, a coalition of Puerto Rican leaders and legal advocacy organizations would serve as the driving force to raise social and political awareness regarding the blatant discrimination toward this population of students. Eventually, this would obligate the school system to provide a culturally and linguistically responsive structure in the city's schools to provide greater equity for Spanish-speaking children.

According to Sonia Nieto (1995), the early literature refers to the "Puerto Rican problem," implying that the educational difficulties of Puerto Rican students were a result of their presumably inferior culture, language, and socioeconomic backgrounds. A 1935 New York State Report entitled "Reactions of the Puerto Rican Children in New York City to Psychological Tests" describes Puerto Rican children in the following way:[42]

> "Puerto Ricans are adding greatly to the already tremendous problem of the intellectually subnormal school retardates of alien parentage, whence are recruited most delinquents and criminals. Indeed, the majority of the Puerto Rican children examined betray a family mentality which should not be permitted admission here, further to deteriorate standards already so seriously impaired by mass immigration of the lowest levels of populations of many nations. Most Puerto Rican children here cannot be assimilated in the existing type of civi-

---

42   New York State Report entitled "Reactions of the Puerto Rican Children in New York City to Psychological Tests. 1935; cited in No. 72 Civ. 4002 United States District Court, S.D. New York.

lization and they are helping to turn the tide back to a lower stage of progress."

The organizations that emerged at the forefront of this fight included ASPIRA, UBP, and the Puerto Rican Legal Defense and Education Fund (PRLDEF).[43] In the context of the struggle for community control and bilingual education, the leaders of these organizations played important roles in the struggle for education and language rights for Puerto Ricans and other communities marginalized by the schools. The two founders of these prominent community organizations, namely ASPIRA and UBP, were frustrated and tired of Puerto Rican parents being blamed for their children's educational problems and lack of achievement.

Dr. Antonia Pantoja and Dr. Evelina Antonetty identified the problem as being not inherent within Puerto Rican students but rather the failure of the school system to provide an equitable education to this population of students. They strategized and reframed the problem as not the lack of intelligence or academic potential of the youth, but rather as the systemic racism that existed within the Board of Education. In 1970 Evelina Lopez Antonetty, the founder of UBP, in testimony before a US Congress Select Committee on Equal Educational Opportunity for Puerto Rican Children, argued: *"The problem is not our Puerto Rican children. The problem is a system of education that squeezes and manipulates and destroys our children. The Federal Government must stop subsidizing this bungling, biased bureaucracy. You must give our communities a chance to educate our children"* (U.S. Senate 1970: 3754).[44]

---

43   Jerald E. Podair, *The Strike that Changed New York. Blacks, Whites, and the Ocean Hill-Brownsville Crisis* (New Haven: Yale University Press, 2002).

44   Aspira of N.Y. v. Bd. of Ed. of City of New York 423 F. Supp. 647 (S.D.N.Y. 1976).

Lopez Antonetty's plea was echoed by Antonia Pantoja, a social worker and the founder of ASPIRA and several other Puerto Rican organizations, who testified about the challenges that Puerto Rican parents and students encountered when engaging the school system:

> *"When you deal with the school system at the administrative level and at the teachers' level, you find a recalcitrant system that will continue to tell you that they are doing things in the ways educators believe best and you are not an educator, and should not meddle into anything they are doing."* (U.S. Senate 1970: 3691)

Pantoja believed that this intransigence, combined with the assimilationist orientation of the schools, was psychologically damaging and viewed it as an assault on the identity and well-being of Puerto Rican children. During her testimony, she stated:

> *"This brings me to the fact that the schools have mounted an attack on the child who speaks Spanish and who is different; an attack to force him to give this up. What happens as a result is that the child is ashamed of himself and his parents, and ashamed of his speaking Spanish. This hurts these children's motivation and ability to learn. Because, you know, if you don't think well of yourself you are not going to able to achieve in the learning of a new language, or in the learning of new skills."* (U.S. Senate 1970: 3688)

Lopez Antonetty and Pantoja's statements reveal their lack of confidence in the white male-dominated Board of Education to produce any meaningful programs or reforms that would motivate and nurture Puerto Rican children:

"We have arrived at the conclusion that they have failed to, and they will never be able to provide certain functions. I refer to such functions as motivation, guidance and programs to develop a positive identity in the children. Those functions, we in the Puerto Rican community can do best for our own children."
(U.S. Senate 1970: 3689)

Dr. Pantoja's and Dr. Lopez Antonetty's testimonies also resonated with African Americans during this period, highlighting that the Board of Education had failed to persuade white parents to voluntarily desegregate and increase access to quality schools for children of color. They concluded that African American and the Puerto Rican communities should have the opportunity to make educational decisions in the interests of their children. After a decade of failure to implement Brown, this perspective gave life to the community control movement and the institutionalization of bilingual education programs for all language minority students in NYC public schools.

ASPIRA is Spanish for "aspire." This nonprofit youth organization was founded by Antonia Pantoja in 1961. From its inception, ASPIRA was dedicated to advancing the Puerto Rican community through educating its youth (Santiago 1978: 5).[45] Its focus was on high school and college retention and was facilitated by ASPIRA clubs, which organized young people and developed leadership at their various high schools and colleges. *Aspirantes* who were student participants in ASPIRA clubs would subsequently organize a sit-in supporting bilingual educational programming and the hiring of bilingual teachers (Reyes 2000: 76).

---

45 Anthony De Jesús and Madeline Perez, "Community Control to Consent Decree: Puerto Ricans Organizing for Education and Language Rights in 60s and 70s New York City."

By the early 1970s, Pantoja and others were beginning to consider legal strategies to institutionalize bilingual education. To achieve this goal, ASPIRA, with a group of Puerto Rican parents, and the Puerto Rican Legal Defense and Education Fund (PRLDEF) filed suit in the US District Court against the Board of Education of New York City in 1972 and won the case on October 22, 1976.[46] Clearly, the Supreme Court's decision on Brown v. Board of Education in 1954 set a strong legal precedent and foundation to pursue the *Aspira Consent Decree of 1972*. In New York City the Aspira Consent Decree would seek to include ELLs as ostensible beneficiaries of the promise of Brown. Although this entitlement initially was for Spanish surname students, the law mandates services for schoolchildren in the NYC public school system, who speak over 150 languages.

I became very passionate about organizing and educating parents about the overrepresentation of Black and Latino students enrolled in special education programs, and the negative stigma attached with the labels being applied to our children, which in many instances became part of the drop-out-to-prison pipeline.

Years before I earned my doctorate at TC, I knew that I needed to build something of value and meaning to my community and to preserve and honor the legacy of struggle and sacrifices made by Dr. Lopez Antonetty and Dr. Pantoja. I had the privilege of meeting and speaking with these two powerful women of integrity who fought for equity in education and the creation of legislation that would guide policy. This policy had a monumental impact on the education of Puerto Rican/Latino students in NYC that would ultimately benefit thousands of immigrant children who were multicultural and linguistically diverse. Their fight and their experiences greatly influenced the path that I have taken throughout my professional life and my dedi-

---

46   Aspira of N.Y. v. Bd. of Ed. of City of New York 423 F. Supp. 647 (S.D.N.Y. 1976).

cation to the education of multilingual and multicultural children. Today hundreds of language groups are protected by the policies and regulations that the Aspira Consent Decree institutionalized in the largest system in the United States.

To me, it only made sense that the time that I invested to earn a doctorate in education needed to be impactful and harness a greater purpose and vision that would include the preservation of the core values and principles that were taught by Dr. Lopez Antonetty and Dr. Antonia Pantoja and this included building institutions that reflected the values that they fought for. In 1985, Dr. Lopez Antonetty passed away suddenly, and our community lost one of its greatest champions and treasures. In 1996, Dr. Pantoja received the Presidential Medal of Freedom from President Bill Clinton.

Dr. Antonia Pantoja receives Presidential Medal of Freedom, White House, 1996. Joined by first lady, Hillary Clinton, and Congresswoman Nydia Velázquez.

CHAPTER 11

DEVELOPING AN EDUCATIONAL PHILOSOPHY

> "Knowledge is the prime need of the hour."
> **—DR. MARY McLEOD BETHUNE**

My educational philosophy was profoundly influenced by philosophers I encountered at TC. Central to these were Horace Mann and John Dewey, whose ideas from the late 1800s and early 1900s were woven into many course requirements. Their teachings shaped my vision for a charter school serving children of color in underserved communities. However, my perspective was not solely influenced by these two figures. I was also inspired by African American luminaries like W. E. B. Du Bois and Dr. Mary Jane McLeod Bethune. Du Bois, a Harvard-educated philosopher and historian, promoted the advancement of African Americans through education, emphasizing the importance of the "Talented Tenth," the top ten percent who would lead and uplift their community.

Dr. Mary Jane McLeod Bethune, the daughter of former slaves, emerged as a pivotal Black educator, civil rights leader, and government official in the twentieth century. Her college set benchmarks for modern Black colleges. As an adviser to President Roosevelt, she championed African American rights. She founded the Daytona Beach Literary and Industrial School for Training Negro Girls, which later merged with Cookman Institute, forming the Bethune-Cookman College in 1929, granting degrees by 1943.

In a 1946 letter, Dr. Bethune expressed her educational philosophy as a "three-fold training of head, hand, heart," emphasizing a comprehensive education grounded in the dignity of labor and spiritual values. She once stated to the American Teachers Association that African Americans would persistently seek equal educational opportunities until all barriers were dissolved.

At TC, the curriculum drew heavily from revered educators like Horace Mann, an educational reformer and abolitionist. Born in 1796, Mann championed public education, believing in its power to uphold a free society. His guiding principles were that education should be public, inclusive, nonsectarian, and imparted by trained professionals.

John Dewey, born October 20, 1859, began his college journey at fifteen years of age in Vermont, eventually obtaining a doctorate from Johns Hopkins. He published over one thousand works, primarily focusing on the ideal education philosophy. For Dewey, education wasn't about aiming for prestigious universities but nurturing students' individual interests. He believed in understanding a child's background and experiences to guide their learning and growth. Dewey stressed that for a democracy to thrive, its citizens must address societal issues collectively, valuing varied opinions. He viewed the learning process as more significant than any specific outcome. According to Hickman,[47] Dewey's pragmatism highlighted "learning by doing," favoring experiential learning over mere memorization. This progressive education theory, emphasizing

---

47   Larry A. Hickman, Stefan Neubert, and Kersten Reich, eds., John Dewey Between Pragmatism and Constructivism (New York: Fordham University Press, 2009).

hands-on, student-centered activities, became foundational at institutions like Bank Street College, where I had studied prior to enrolling at TC.

In the Project or Problem Method, which Dewey advocated, the child's interests and purposes are the most important things. Problem-Based Learning (PBL),[48] for example, a method used widely in education today, incorporates Dewey's ideas pertaining to learning through active inquiry.

What resonated with me as a young educator was Dewey's learner-centered approach. He envisioned education as fostering critical, reflective, and engaged individuals, contrasting the prevalent rote learning. Dewey's perspective on integrating traditional subjects with a learner's interests significantly influenced our charter high school's curriculum design and the process for teaching and learning in an optimal learning environment by incorporating content-rich materials throughout all content areas that provide challenging and meaningful experiences.

This philosophy permeated our teaching methods, emphasizing engaging lessons, critical questioning, and project-based learning, especially in science and mathematics. He rejected the rote-learning approach driven by predetermined curriculum, which was the standard teaching method when I became a teacher in the South Bronx. According to the literature, while he used the term "progressive education," this has since been misappropriated to describe, in some cases, a hands-off approach to children's learning, which was not what Dewey proposed. Dewey believed that traditional subject matter was important but should be integrated with the strengths and interests of the learner.[49]

---

48   "Interdisciplinary Journal of Problem-Based Learning," Purdue e-Pubs, accessed January 20, 2024, https://docs.lib.purdue.edu/ijpbl/.

49   Sonia E. Murrow, *Preparing Teachers to Remake Society: New College at Teachers College* (Columbia University, 1932-1939).

CHAPTER 12

THE *POLITICS* OF EDUCATION REFORM

"The manifestation of a promise of God may be delayed but His word tells us it is not denied."

—2 CORINTHIANS 1:20

I t was 2004, and there were New York State and citywide reports that the DOE would soon start dismantling comprehensive NYC high schools. Most of the high schools, particularly in the Bronx, were overcrowded and yielding very low achievement results as well as poor graduation rates. In addition, these schools were on the persistently dangerous and unsafe schools list. There were numerous incidents of gang violence, weapons and drug possession, and it was necessary to increase metal detectors and school safety officers who would be employed by the New York Police Department (NYPD). This birthed the advent of the new and small schools' movement that was part of the larger vision for educational reform.

The local CSDs started releasing Request for Proposals (RFPs) for a twenty-first century grant that would allow educators and organizations to submit a concept and theme for new schools. This was presented as a public process open to all who qualified, in order to reimagine the delivery of education for high school and middle school students.

I was excited about having the chance to put my vision on paper! Every evening, no matter how long my day had been, I would work on a concept that was aligned with the design for a school that I wanted to create. The proposal had to be written into a format that followed the guidelines and the format they required. My focus was to develop a proposal for a small high school that would be rigorous in its academic standards, as well as one that would integrate the arts and sciences throughout all content areas. This was it! The opportunity that I had been waiting for. I knew immediately that there was no option. I had to do this. The timeline between the application and interview process was a short one. In three months or less we had to develop a team that would include educators, businesspeople, parents, and members of the community who would be invited to a meeting to defend the proposal. Several aspects of the process were unclear and there were organizations and individuals who seemed to have "inside" information connected to the decision-makers and a political advantage that we did not have. Despite the obvious challenges, I moved forward and prepared the team that I assembled with determination and optimism.

Notwithstanding the difficulty of preparing a submission that would fit the voluminous guidelines, the process was also riddled with political dynamics. There would be a highly subjective selection of teams that would be moved forward and those who would be rejected. A fellow colleague commented to me years later that the process was like that of a beauty pageant. The experience would be largely influenced by those who were well connected to the sociopolitical stratosphere. I was not an insider, although very familiar with CSD 10 politics and its superintendent as well as Bronx politics. The teachers' union and the Office of New Schools were also prominent in their participation as to the decisions that would be made at every orientation and interview. There would be ten applications and teams selected from hundreds of submissions that would be moved forward.

It was a competitive process, and I was eager to succeed. I had earned my doctorate in education administration a decade earlier and completed the process for the Principal's License and Education Administrators credentials. Although in hindsight I must admit that in the first round of submissions, we were not ready. It was a rushed proposal without much time between revisions to reflect and produce a well-written and quality document.

I continued to pursue the process and meticulously followed the guidelines. This would include an application review, team interviews, and an assessment of the team capacity, with clarifying questions followed by a waiting period. After the interviews and a rubric that was never provided, we were rejected and asked to resubmit our application when the process reopened. We did so and our proposal was rejected yet again. The rationale that was provided did not make sense and was rooted in political favoritism and district politics and the biases that were at play. I was so heartbroken that I must have sobbed for an entire afternoon. I was very discouraged, but within three days I started working again to find another pathway. I was resolute that these rejections were not going to crush the vision that God had placed in my heart.

In 2004, still deeply committed to my vision, I invited the key stakeholders from the community and the district to tour an abandoned building on Jerome Avenue and West 181 Street, envisioning it as our school's location. Believing in possibilities, I hoped that the DOE could refurbish the site. My enthusiasm may have seemed unrealistic to some, especially when we inspected the dilapidated building. The superintendent, impeccably dressed, might have questioned my judgment, but she remained courteous throughout.

With the district facing space issues, I wondered: Why not utilize this structure? Despite its evident wear, I imagined bustling classrooms. Reflecting two decades later, I realize my zeal could have been premature. Yet, the challenges and countless meetings to rally support paved the way for my next endeavor: founding a charter school from the ground up. The overcrowded school district needed spaces to renovate. While I envisioned transforming a dilapidated building into classrooms, my ambitious dream was ahead of its time. I rode the wave of opposition and these challenges paved the way for starting a charter school.

A decade prior, I had defended my dissertation at TC. But the complexity of starting a charter school, with its educational politics and scrutiny, was unparalleled. My experience with Bronx politics and the machinations of CSD 10 prepared me for the intense challenges with the New York City Department of Education (NYCDOE) and NYSED. Originally, I had no plans to deviate from the NYC public school system, having begun my journey there.

Now, when I objectively reflect twenty years later, it is clear to me that the desire to pursue my vision and dream for a school was too ambitious for the time. But I realized later that all the efforts—numerous meetings to garner political support for this project and failed appeals for reconsideration—were merely setbacks that set me up for the second most rigorous process that I have ever voluntarily engaged in.

Ironically it was never my intention to work outside of the existing NYC system of public schools. After all, I started out as a paraprofessional in the school system in 1977 and started teaching in 1980, working my way up the ladder of ambition to education administrator. I paid for numerous exams just to be considered highly qualified to supervise faculty and lead schools in the NYC public school system.

However, I recognized the teacher's union's influence, which often upheld mediocrity, negatively impacting many students of color. Despite the pushback, I was determined to open a charter school that emphasized excellence and inclusion. My vision was unwavering: a school where every student succeeded and was college ready. Facing opposition only fueled my resolve. By 2005, I embarked on the charter school movement, working tirelessly on an application for a school that would launch in 2006.

Fortunately, it became clear that any attempt to open a school within the existing structure was going to be controlled by the teacher's union that had, to begin with, largely contributed to the crisis of the miseducation of countless students of color in the NYC public schools. This miseducation was caused by the policy of supporting and perpetuating mediocrity among teachers who have full protection by the UFT, making it nearly impossible for any educator or administrator with a vision for excellence to replace teachers with more effective ones in order to provide a high-quality education. My personal history of activism and organizing for civil and human rights, in coalition with numerous union leaders in the 1980s and 1990s to oppose the oppressive and racially hostile anti-immigrant policies and English-only legislation that were being proposed at the time, became somewhat of a paradox as I had organized side by side with union leaders since 1983 on a whole array of educational issues, regressive immigration policies, and English-only legislation. I worked closely with leaders from District Council (DC) 37, DC 65 United Automobiles Union (UAW), 1199, and the Labor Council for Latin American Advancement (LCLAA). However, from my perspective, the UFT, which I was a dues paying member of, was a whole different world that carried questionable baggage and practices, where it is almost impossible to terminate a low-performing teacher who is miseducating children of color living in poverty. To develop and improve a teacher's practice without interference is unheard of. Undeniably, teachers are the first line of defense in our school system and deserve raises and fair treatment. However, does it make sense to place teachers in the same category as nonmanual laborers? Historically, union leaders exist to protect the rights of their "workers," and many workers are oppressed, and rightfully deserve fair living wages and health benefits. However, the fact is that teachers straight out of college will receive salaries that are far beyond the standard working wage as compared with most workers represented by the trades and traditional labor unions.[50] Furthermore, NYC public school teachers work ten months out of the year, with a very generous amount of paid summer vacation time and numerous paid holidays throughout the year with annual salaries that start upward of $75,000. By contrast, at most charter schools that are nonunionized, teachers can be rewarded for their outstanding performance, treated as professionals, and respected for their dedication while receiving a competitive salary and pay raises.

This less than adequate approach to student achievement still exists today in many schools throughout the NYC public school district. The effects of poor methods of teaching and learning are consistently reflected in the poor student achievement results of Latino, African American, Southeast Asian, and Caribbean students throughout the five boroughs.

Although fundamentally I knew that delay was not denial, I had a larger vision that could not be compromised. I probably would have

---

50   Jerald E. Podair, *The Strike that Changed New York. Blacks, Whites, and the Ocean Hill-Brownsville Crisis* (New Haven: Yale University Press, 2002).

not ever have considered opening a charter school if the system had been more open to diversity, equity, and inclusion to make room for a strong-willed, outspoken, visionary Latina leader. I was passionate about the creation of a school that would strive for excellence, where failure was not an option, and where every student achieved, graduated on time, and was prepared for college. Nothing could stop me! There was a great deal of opposition to my bold thinking and determined style of leadership. The audacity of my idea that I could implement a vision and do a better job than the school system was doing at the time would baffle as well as infuriate many in positions of educational leadership and authority. It would turn out that all things do work together for good, and this opposition became a blessing. Just a few years later in 2005, I decided that I would seriously pursue the opportunities that existed within the highly controversial charter school movement. I diligently began working on an application for a charter school that would open on September 11, 2006.

CHAPTER 13

THE POLITICS OF STARTING A CHARTER SCHOOL IN NEW YORK CITY

"Education is the only billion-dollar industry that tolerates abject failure."

—GEOFFREY CANADA

According to Sparks (2021),[51] the charter school movement proceeded to gain traction on both sides of the aisle in the late 1980s and early 1990s, at which point a consensus had developed that public schools in America were failing. Secretary of Education T. H. Bell created the National Commission on Excellence in Education on August 26, 1981, directing it to examine the quality of education in the United States and to make a report to the nation and to him within eighteen months of its first meeting. *A Nation at Risk* (1983)[52] presented evidence of plummeting student performance and argued that such

---

51   Daniel Sparks, *School Board Privatization: A Case Study of New York City Charter Schools* (New York: Columbia University, 2021).

52   US Department of Education, *The Nation at Risk: The Imperative of Educational Reform* (1983).

decline was harmful not only for students and families but for US economic competitiveness in the global economy as well. The foundational ideas of school choice remained integral to the Reagan and Bush administrations' education reform strategy: increased choice and competition, decentralization, and a more involved role of the private sector.

In 2004, the New York City Mayor Michael Bloomberg took control of the public school system. He was a billionaire and philanthropist, and a staunch supporter of charter schools. He appointed a former attorney, Joel Klein,[53] as chancellor of the largest school system in the country,[54] who would lead the NYCDOE to collaborate with organizations and individuals who were interested in the creation of ten additional charter schools. There were already 190 charter schools operating in NYC. All charter applicants were required to participate in numerous orientations that were hosted at the New York City Charter Center, in collaboration with the NYCDOE.

If one was fortunate enough to get through the maze of bureaucracy and the gatekeepers who were strategically placed at every step of the process, this would then require approval by the NYCDOE and the NYSED. The conference rooms were filled with representatives of the various authorizing groups and charter advocacy organizations. In addition, there were numerous passionate, bright-eyed, and motivated educators and administrators who represented various organizations throughout the city who were ready to work harder than they had ever worked in their lives to compete for one of the last charter school slots that would be awarded.

There was one common thread among all applicants that went beyond idealism: the desire to take part in and engage in ground-

---

53   Joel Klein, *Lessons of Hope: How to Fix Our Schools* (Harper, 2014).

54   Ibid.

breaking entrepreneurial high-impact initiatives that would provide a viable alternative to the failing schools in the NYC public school system, which continued to disenfranchise poor children of color. Public schools were failing students and the nation. What started as a bold idea and an experiment twenty-five years ago clearly presented a pathway for educators and visionaries to create independent autonomous schools with an opportunity to design academic programs, control budgets and school finances, and with the ability to hire their own teachers and become their own school district and local education agencies (LEAs).

Ember Reichgott Junge[55] was the Minnesota state senator who authored the law. The 105th Congress of the US House of Representatives introduced HR 2616 to amend the Elementary and Secondary Education Act of 1965 to create charter school legislation and the bill passed with the support of the US Senate. Shortly thereafter, the New York State Charter Act was established. The Charter Schools Movement had already sent shockwaves throughout the nation and challenged the monopoly and influence of the American Federation of Teachers, in New York, since charter schools could operate without collective bargaining structures in place.

Initially the Charter Schools Movement was proposed as part of a larger strategy for national education reform and a launching pad for the voucher system that parents could use to pay for tuition at private and religious institutions. This received broad support from mostly conservative Republicans in 1998. This gave charter schools the reputation of being a highly controversial bipartisan initiative from the starting gate.[56] Today, twenty-five years later, there are over

---

55   Reichgott Junge, Embertt. *Zero Chance of Passage: The Pioneering Charter School Story.* (Edina: Beaver's Pond Press, 2012).

56   H.R.2616 - Charter School Expansion Act of 1998, https://www.congress.gov/bill/105th-congress/house-bill/2616/.

two hundred charter schools operating in NYS that are flourishing. Despite the huge success of charter schools, and the fact that they are public schools that only receive 80 percent of funding as compared with NYC public school districts, they continue to be mischaracterized by the opposition as an effort to privatize education and a plot to siphon funds from the public school system.

The NYC Charter Center was established in 2004 and funded by three foundations—the Tiger Fund, Robin Hood, and the Pumpkin Foundation—that pledged $140 million to support the development of charter schools. The then chancellor, Joel Klein, had a seat on its Board of Directors. I attended a meeting at the charter center to review the criteria and application process for starting a charter school in New York State. In attendance were representatives from the three authorizing entities, which included the NYCDOE, NYSED, and SUNY CSI.

The conference room was filled with about forty aspiring charter school operators. I hung on to every word and took copious notes. I was excited that this could really be the opportunity that I was waiting for to create a mission- and purpose-driven charter high school that would focus on providing immigrant first-generation students with an academically rigorous education that would prepare them for college. The charter school's movement, although controversial and not supported by either the progressive left or most Democrats, presented an avenue for those like me to start a school that was independent and autonomous from the public school system. I was neither a republican nor a conservative and was active in progressive social causes and community activism. I was also greatly influenced by community leaders from the left who had socialist values, as well as independent thinkers with revolutionary ideals.

Despite the appearance of "selling out" to what was considered a right-wing conservative conspiracy, I knew it was the only way forward. I had to drown out those voices as this idea of establishing a charter school was a brilliant and viable path for those like me who wanted to influence change in how Black and Brown children were being educated. This was a unique opportunity to offer an alternative for parents, with the promise of a rigorous and high-quality education for their children with higher education as an aspirational goal. This concept held many possibilities for creating a school rooted in the community that welcomed parent support and input.

TONY LÓPEZ

Tony López and I met in the mid-1980s when we were both activists and volunteers in the NCPRR. It was not until the late 1990s that we realized that we were soulmates, and we started our relationship after a chance encounter in Puerto Rico. We have been happily married since 2001 and continue to serve in mission-aligned and purpose-driven work, serving the community in providing an equitable education to children of color. Tony often reflects on his relationship with Joe Reich who was an important stakeholder in the history of the charter school's movement in New York City:

I met Joe and Carol Reich at El Puente in Williamsburg, Brooklyn in September 1987, the first month I worked as the NYC Director of Support Services for philanthropist Eugene Lang's national "I Have a Dream" Foundation. Joe and Carol now joined 10 other married couples in sponsoring an entire group of graduating elementary school students at least through high school and possibly college with scholarship support. Their IHAD sponsorship was the first project I supported throughout the five-year journey that led me to become NYC's first Executive Director by my late twenties. The year before, I served on security detail for the National Congress for Puerto Rican Rights' March Against the Wall—a protest against the NYBOE's acquiescence to the Hasidic community in Williamsburg in separating black and brown children, from Hasidic children within Public School 16.

Fourteen years later, Joe, Carol, and I would reconnect again. For as long as I knew Elaine, she always dreamed of creating a school. After three failed attempts to create one through the former NYCBOE, she came home one day with a pamphlet from the newly formed NYC Center for Charter School Excellence announcing a call to create a charter school under a new mayor who now controlled NYC's public school system—the NYDOE. Skeptical at first, I reviewed the pamphlet and saw that Joe Reich was the Chairperson of this new organization. I reached out and scheduled a meeting with him. After greeting Carol, I met with Joe and told him "I'm here to be a good husband. My wife has a dream to create a school, I want to support her and I need your support." *The rest is history.*

JOE AND CAROL REICH

In 2012, Joe and Carol Reich published *Getting to Bartlett Street*[57]—a book that tells their story on how they embarked upon a journey to start a charter school in New York. In the section on "New Way Forward: Charter Schools," Carol Reich writes:

> *"Nobody expected an easy road [CE1] when it came to passing the New York State charter schools act, as Governor Pataki would later explain to us. Virtually no one in the state legislature was firmly on his side. The Republicans, by and large, did not like the idea, he told us, because they were primarily focused on securing additional funds for suburban school districts they represented. The Democrats didn't like it because they received most of their financial support from the teachers unions. The teachers unions didn't like it because it threatened their status quo in conventional public schools. Tenure is granted to virtually all teachers, and it is very rare that a 10-year teacher is fired. There is also very little monetary incentive for teachers to work harder than is necessary because union contracts prohibit incentive pay. Also, very few public schools have been closed for poor performance or mismanagement. Charter schools turn every one of those ideas on their heads. Should a charter school not achieve the goals set out in their charter, they could be, and often were, closed. Should teachers or administrators not perform well, they could be fired. It was, therefore, not surprising that Pataki's proposal was met with fierce opposition in Albany. The Democrats, who controlled the state legislature, joined the teachers union and school administrators in championing the status quo and blocked Pataki's charter*

---

57   Joe Reich and Carol Reich, "Getting to Bartlett Street: our 25 year quest to level the playing field in education," 2012, https://ssir.org/books/excerpts/entry/getting_to_bartlett_street_our_25_year_quest_to_level_the_playing_field_in#.

law. But Pataki wasn't about to give up, and Joe and I found it almost entertaining to watch the governor tango toward a deal with the Democrats that December. More brazen it could not have been. Legislators had spent a lot of time and effort for a law to raise their salaries from $59,500 to $79,500 on January 1st, 1999. If pay raise was not passed in December, 1998, then the legislation could not receive their raise for two more years. Pataki made it clear that he was ready to veto the pay raise unless, of course, a deal could be struck. Brazen as it may have been, but we learned that this is how business gets done in New York. In the end, the salary of the legislators was increased to $79,500, and the children of New York got a charter school law allowing for the creation of 100 charter schools."

LATINO LEADERS AND THE CHARTER SCHOOLS MOVEMENT

At the time that we applied for our charter school, there were less than a handful of charter schools being led by Latino educators and community-based organizations. This included a charter school founded by Dr. Bishop Raymond Rivera, founder of the Latino Pastoral Action Center (LPAC), who is a progressive spiritual leader and oversees the council of holistic ministries in New York, and a former parent organizer from East Harlem. Bishop Rivera is a highly regarded pastor, theologian, and author, as well as a leader of holistic ministries and principles of liberation theology.[58] In 2001, Bishop launched the Family Life Academy Charter Schools (FLACS) in the southwest Bronx in CSD 9, which grew into a highly successful, well-respected

---

58   Raymond Rivera, Set the Captives Free (New York: Knopf, 2023).

community-grown charter network of four schools in the Bronx. It has received national accolades under the leadership of his wife, Marilyn Calo, a former administrator from CSD 4 in East Harlem.

Then there is Amber Charter School that was founded in 2000 by the Association of Community Progressive Dominicans (ACDP) whose founder was Guillermo Linares. Luis Miranda, a community leader from the progressive sector[59] who in the 1980s and 1990s organized parents to register to vote and to fight for equity in education alongside Guillermo, was a young

Planning Board Meeting: Dr. Guillermo Linares and Dr. Ruíz López photographed with Luis Garden Acosta, former member of YLP and founder of El Puente

Dominican charismatic community leader from Washington Heights. He was the first community school board member of Latino heritage and Dominican descent to be voted onto CSD 6 that historically had an all-white majority board in a community that was steadily growing in its immigrant population. Guillermo had political aspirations and would later become the first Dominican elected to public office in New York City and later elected to the New York State Assembly. Today Amber has grown into a highly successful community-grown model with three schools operating in East Harlem, Kingsbridge, and Inwood.

59

It is important to note that Guillermo was one of my very first mentors in community organizing and the politics of education. We met at IS 184 when I was a bilingual education teacher associate while studying at CCNY in 1978. He encouraged me to participate on a panel that he organized on bilingual education and the impact that the budget cuts would have on the teacher preparation programs such as BPS that I was part of. It was my very first panel presentation and introduction to community organizing and activism.

THE NYC CHARTER CENTER FOR EXCELLENCE

In 2005, I applied to the NYC Charter Center for Excellence for a planning grant of $30,000 and an opportunity to incubate in their office spaces for one year. This meant that I would have access to a cubicle and a phone, as well as the opportunity to participate in workshops and technical assistance meetings on all the financial, governance, and business areas of operating a charter school. This open door provided me with a unique experience to collaborate with colleagues who also were competing to win one of the few charter slots available. The initial charter grant would assist with expenses toward various aspects of a charter school back-office start-up. Their offices were in the Wall Street area at 111 Broadway at Trinity Place. I remember the daily commute well, a stressful drive from the northwest Bronx to lower Manhattan in heavy traffic, at times more than one hour each way, then circling endlessly for parking in a large municipal lot. But this was a small sacrifice to pursue the dream.

In the fall of 2004, I began writing and submitted the first application to the NYCDOE with copies of half a dozen binders that were mailed via FEDEX to the offices of the NYSED in Albany, New York. We were expected to engage in the grueling process of writing eight sections of an application that included an executive summary, an educational philosophy, the academic program, proposed assessments, a staffing plan, a governance section, bylaws, a finance plan, and a first-year line-item budget. After having completed the application, the submission instructions required the preparation of five copies of binders with approximately five hundred pages of documents in each, not counting attachments for curriculum crosswalks, which is what we know today as curriculum maps, for every content area, signed assurances and resumes for members of the planning team who would later become board members.

This application was revised and resubmitted at least three times and every time the authorizers at both the DOE and the NYSED kept finding something they did not like, or a page. Instead of just requesting that section or page, I was told that they wanted all binders resubmitted again. I was physically and mentally exhausted and found it hard to believe they would make such a demand. This pushback was clearly intended to discourage applicants and to weed out the weak from the strong. However, I was persistent, and failure was not an option for me. This was a test in endurance, so I dutifully followed instructions and continued to send the binders that were requested. After the second time it was clear that there was not a good faith effort to make the process easier and it appeared to be intentionally difficult.

The personalities of the people working at the NYSED division where these applications were being received and reviewed and read were no less problematic. The expenses for making copies at a local Kinkos in Manhattan were out of pocket and costly. The collection and sorting of materials were time-consuming, and the repetitive tasks were extremely frustrating. I did not have an assistant and often found myself working by myself until late into the night in the office that I set up at the living room table. This experience far exceeded the level of mental and emotional strain that I experienced with the demanding completion of my dissertation and its defense.

This scenario was different due to the multiple political games and various levels of Machiavellian dynamics that were evident to most who were paying attention. These political war games were being carried out by multiple bad actors at the DOE, technocrats at the NYSED, and the dynamics of the NYC Charter Center. There was a coalition of gatekeepers who were actively attempting to block our product from being seen and received by the commissioner and the NYS Board of Regents. My husband Tony, who was working at the NYC Charter Center for Excellence as the Vice President for Leadership, had remained neutral for the entire process and would recuse himself from any conversations that involved our proposed charter school. However, he had enough, observing the abuse from the sidelines and stepped in to assist with the politics of this process and to advocate for our application based on the merits and the fact that we had resubmitted the application several times while others who had weaker applications were being put forward. We were both committed to submitting a successful product that would be approved. It appeared that our application had a target on it and our application was not favored. We were faced with frequent decision points, and Tony and I agreed that I could not quit.

After two consecutive years of working on the application during Thanksgiving and Christmas holidays, perfecting sections, contending with two letters of rejection accompanied by requests to resubmit three full applications multiple times, attending two panel interviews at the NYCDOE, and engaging community leaders to advocate for our application, we were finally approved to go to the next round of recommendations to the NYSED in the fall of 2005. The buzz was that if successful and accepted at this level of the process, our charter application would be recommended as part of the ten applications that would be reviewed and put forward for a vote by the NYS Board of Regents.

COMPETING FOR THE LAST CHARTER SPOT: JANUARY 2006

On October 31, 2005, a letter was sent from the Office of Portfolio Schools at the NYCDOE to former Commissioner Dr. Sheila Evans-Tranumn that began, "It is my pleasure to send to you an approved application for International Leadership Charter School…"

The letter came from the desk of Chancellor Klein and contained a proposed charter agreement for my signature. I was elated yet cautiously optimistic. Was this really happening? After two and a half years of persistence, my vision for the first charter high school in the Bronx would finally become a reality! We were moving forward. However, there was still one more step in the process. The NYS Commissioner's office had to submit an official recommendation to the Board of Regents for a vote. This is where the process became more vicious in nature. I was really swimming with the sharks now!

As the December deadline came closer for a decision to be made, there was a great deal of anxiety as well as political strategies and war games taking place behind the scenes. I was reminded by a friend and well-respected community and social justice activist that what we did have was social capital. He reminded me that as an educator, former organizer, and activist, while I did not have the financial resources, I

THE NEW YORK CITY DEPARTMENT OF EDUCATION
JOEL I. KLEIN, *Chancellor*

OFFICE OF NEW SCHOOLS
52 Chambers Street, Room 405, New York, NY 10007
Phone: 212-374-5419   Fax: 212-374-5581

October 31, 2005

Ms. Shelia Evans-Tranumn
Associate Commissioner
New York State Education Department
55 Hanson Place, Room 400
Brooklyn, NY 11217

Re: International Leadership Charter School

Dear Commissioner Evans-Tranumn:

It is my pleasure to send to you an approved application for the International Leadership Charter School.

On September 1, 2005, the New York City Department of Education ("NYCDOE") received the attached proposal from Elaine Ruiz-Lopez, the lead applicant for International Leadership Charter School. The NYCDOE conducted a rigorous and comprehensive review of this application. This review included a detailed analysis of the proposed school's education program, business plan, and governance structure by a panel of NYCDOE staff as well as charter school experts. Furthermore, the participation of a representative from the State Education Department provided important insight and consistency to our deliberations.

Based on the analysis of the proposal and requested modifications, the NYCDOE finds that:

    a. This proposed charter school meets the requirements set out in The New York Charter Schools Act (Article 56 of the New York State Consolidated Education Law), and other applicable laws, rules and regulations;

    b. The applicant has demonstrated the ability to operate the proposed charter school in an educationally and fiscally sound manner; and that

    c. Granting the application is likely to improve student learning and achievement and materially further the purposes of §2850(2) of Article 56.

On October 31, 2005, Chancellor Klein approved this application and delivered to Elaine Ruiz-Lopez a signed proposed charter agreement. Elaine Ruiz-Lopez signed this proposed charter agreement and pursuant to §2852(4) of the Charter Schools Act, the NYCDOE is submitting to the State Board of Regents, for final approval and issuance, a copy of International Leadership Charter School proposed charter agreement and the approved school's application.

Subject to the instructions from your Office, two copies are being sent to Lisa Long and six copies to Carol Wallace. Thank you for your attention to this matter and please do not hesitate to contact me if you have any questions in this regard.

Sincerely,

M. ashn

Mashea M. Ashton
Executive Director, Office of Charter Schools

had the full support of the people in my community who were behind me in this effort. I shifted my focus to educating the parents and future school community on the mission, vision, and the process for receiving an approval from the NYS Board of Regents and the educational benefits that this college prep learning environment would deliver to high school-age children. My political activist friend and mentor, Luis Garden Acosta, was right, I was a Bronx native with strong values as an educator. He went on to say that I had more credibility with the parent community than those whose boards were connected to foundation and corporate support. We took his advice and proceeded with confidence. The charter school's office staff at the DOE in consultation with the NYC Charter Center were calling the shots. They were empowered to make their recommendations on which applications would move forward. The groups that had the leverage were those who had boards with deep pockets and connected to foundations and money to invest from the start.

I was fifty years of age and had already dedicated more than half of my life to fighting alongside community leaders who advocated for improvements and reform in the school system. The support for our high school came primarily from the will of the parents and the community, who signed petitions to justify the need for our charter school. The community was ready for a change and an alternative to the failing high schools in CSD 10. The eighteen groups who submitted applications were lobbying the city and the state representatives, the authorizers, and the NYS Board of Regents and those in power to receive one of the ten coveted charters left to be authorized in the state of New York.

Our planning board consisted of a teacher, a banker and business-person, a former executive director of a community-based organization who ran a high school alternative program, a director of international programs at the YMCA, a parent, and me. We met numerous times and prepared for the interview to become familiar with the questions and how to respond to the challenges we would be facing in starting a new charter high school for Bronx youth—who were first-generation immigrants, poor, and economically disadvantaged—and give them the chance to escape the failing middle schools. We knew that we had to fight for this charter spot, as there was too much at stake.

As a Puerto Rican woman, it has been my experience that I have always had to work harder than the white males of privilege. This process crystallized inequity and favoritism. The team at the NYC Chancellor's Office of Charter Schools decided that I did not fit the profile of a school leader they could "dance" with, or have what it takes to establish a school operation and lead a successful charter school. We had been part of the process for a few years by then, and eventually the decision-makers took notice of our passion, drive, endurance, and our commitment to the Bronx community that we were proposing to serve. We were not taking no for an answer!

In the end, there actually was a benefit of having to write, submit, revise, and resubmit sections of our application multiple times. As a result, we had a product that was of high quality and a design that was well developed, which has carried our charter school through three renewals over the past eighteen years. I was confident even at this early stage that we had the advantage over the other applications submitted. Although not a strong criterion in the process, some of the lead applicants were non-educators with strong professional credentials, but had never supervised teachers, led a school, or were familiar with curriculum, teaching, and learning. Would their background be acceptable for those who had the power to make the decision?

I should not have been surprised at what happened next, since at every turn they were trying to block our charter school. Despite having received a letter from the charter school's office that the recommendation was made to SED to move forward for the vote by the NYS Board of Regents, shortly thereafter there was an aggressive and targeted plan by the charter school's office at the DOE during Christmas time to rescind the recommendation. It became clear that the gatekeepers who were preventing our charter school from moving forward included the leadership at the NYC Charter Center at the time, the staff at the Charter Schools Office at DOE, and the overpaid technocrats at SED who had not yet given up on their biased plan to stop us from establishing the first charter high school in the Bronx.

We were triangulated from all sides, but we were ready for them this time. We were cash poor but indeed rich in social capital. Our qualifications, history of work, and reputation in defending the rights of the marginalized to have access to a quality education as a civil rights hand already preceded us. Our grassroots activism and work in education gave us credibility in the community and with some of the Latino political leaders of influence. For three years we labored over this application and dutifully followed the process and wrote and rewrote and implemented recommendations made that were intended to be busy work to derail our plans. At the eleventh hour as January 2006 approached, we knew that this was our final shot and we desperately needed political support.

I give all the credit to my husband Tony—my silent cofounder who proceeded to make phone calls to all our friends and stakeholders at the state level and one person who became our champion in this fight (NYS Board of Regents Lorraine Cortez-Vasquez who later was appointed as the NY Secretary of State). She is a very well-known and highly regarded

Lorraine Cortez-Vasquez

Puerto Rican woman in Bronx politics, and former executive director of ASPIRA from 1992 to 1996. Tony was hired by Lorraine as her deputy executive director. When Lorraine moved on for a life in government and politics in 1996, he became the organization's new executive director. Lorraine Cortez Vasquez is currently the New York state commissioner for the Department of the Aging.

Tony had enough, and was ready to expose the corruption and arbitrary nature of the charter school application process being led by the DOE and SED, who responded to our application with eighty-eight questions for clarification. Once we did, they followed up with forty-four, then twenty-two, and the weekend before the vote, a question we already answered as part of the original eighty-eight.

The discrimination in the process was obvious to all. Who gets to decide how and by whom our children are educated? Most applicants were white, and I was one of two lead applicants of color. Many of the groups had attorneys sitting on their boards who had connections to people with influence, deep pockets, strong foundation ties, and relationships to the authorizers and leadership at the charter center. By contrast, our team consisted of two educators, a principal, a nonprofit executive, and a businessman. We prepared for the interviews and became familiar with the questions and how to respond to the challenges we would be facing in starting a new charter high school for Bronx youth, who were first-generation immigrants, economically disadvantaged, and from failing middle schools. I was confident that we had the advantage over the applications submitted.

Although not a strong criterion in the process, some of the lead applicants were non-educators who had never supervised teachers, led a school, or were familiar with curriculum, teaching, and learning. But would it be enough for those making the decision? This is where the value of preserving relationships rings true.

CHAPTER 14

THE CHARTER SCHOOL START-UP: EIGHT MONTHS TO OPENING

> "Be careful about what you set your heart
> upon for it will surely be yours."
> —JAMES BALDWIN

We had won the victory and the official vote by the NYS Board of Regents, with authorization from the state to move forward and create a charter school from "*nada*" (scratch). We had all of eight months to prepare for full charter school operations that included identifying a space to lease and operate from, painting, renovations, student enrollment, buying furniture, interviewing, hiring faculty, security, maintenance staff contracts, securing insurance policies, purchasing textbooks and classroom supplies, and installing security systems and phone lines. To be in full compliance with strong governance and oversight, we also had to identify and build a Board of Trustees.

All of this had to be accomplished with limited finances and 80 percent of the allocation for each public school student. I was then fifty years old and had already worked in the field of education for the past twenty-nine years in various roles from teacher, college professor, to school administrator. There was a sense of urgency and intensity in the work every day, and I had never worked as hard or as long. Oddly, it never felt like work! I was living my calling and educating children who looked like me and who were mostly from the Bronx. They had dreams just as I did as a child, and this further fueled my passion to provide the tools that they needed to be successful.

We had limited choices and some groups were being granted colocated space from the DOE. However, we had already decided that this was not an option for us. It would not have allowed for the type of school culture that we wanted to create, one that would be independent from an NYC public school facility. This would allow us to avoid having to contend with the building-based politics.

I searched throughout the catchment area for where we wanted to locate our charter school, and I found what I thought was the perfect opportunity. Perfect, until the landlord, who was part of a Bronx-based real estate company, requested that we make a $10,000 contribution to the Bronx Borough President's incumbent reelection campaign in 2005. When we were approached a second time to contribute, we became very uncomfortable and recognized this as extortion. Fortunately, this brought into question the potential problems of entering into a lease with this company. We did not have a large amount of disposable income, and the funds that would be allocated were public dollars. Such a donation would be not only irresponsible but also an act of malfeasance to invest public dollars to doing so. After this old-fashioned shakedown and nearly one year of engagement and attending shady events, reviewing plans for renovations, we severed our ties with them.

In April of 2006 there were still no alternative prospects for a site to operate from. But then, God closed a door and opened a window! After I had attended a church service with my family, we drove through the Marble Heights/Kingsbridge neighborhood. Suddenly I spotted an advertisement for rental space at 2900 Exterior Street. It was just five months before opening! I immediately contacted the landlord and requested a walkthrough. It was exactly the space that we needed to get started. I realized that God was watching over our charter school.

We ran into several challenges after leasing the building, beginning with issues pertaining to an installation we had to make on the school site. It was the charter school's responsibility to design and build a fire alarm system that would communicate directly with the fire department. To occupy the space as a school operation, we required a mayoral zoning override to make it legal to operate a school. After submitting an override and several meetings with the assistant commissioner's office at the Bronx DOB, and thorough reviews of our safety and egress plans, and the assistance of Deputy Mayor Dennis Walcott, we received the official letter of approval for the zoning override, from Mayor Bloomberg's office.

We were fighting challenges up until the last minute. Our Temporary Certificate of Occupancy (TCO) was actually issued at the eleventh hour, the Friday before the scheduled school opening on Monday, September 11, 2006. The countless efforts, meetings, and sleepless nights leading up to this new beginning started to bring the dream into focus. The real work of creating a high-quality learning environment that was academically rigorous and uniquely different from the failing schools surrounding us was finally able to begin.

Our team of four remained on board during the summer months, meticulously laying out designs for classrooms, painting the school walls with our signature sky blue and navy-blue colors, and outfitting our rooms with brand new furniture, white boards, SMART Boards, teacher desks, makeshift racks for outer clothing, and turning a former computer lab into a cafeteria. We ordered custom signs with the name of our school prominently displayed on the outside of our building. We were now ready for the christening of our school!

On Monday, September 11, 2006, we had a ribbon-cutting ceremony and successfully opened our doors ready to welcome seventy-seven incoming high school students. Our parents, six founding teachers, students, operations staff, and members of the Board of Trustees were present. There was jubilation and the electrifying promise of change could be felt in the air. In attendance was Lorraine Cortez-Vasquez, Secretary of the State of New York and former

member of the NYS Board of Regents, appointed by former Bronx Borough President Adolfo Carrion to represent the Bronx.

The backbone of any school operation is its staff. There must be a reliance on highly qualified and well-prepared faculty. In the short amount of time that we had to prepare classrooms for the opening, we needed to identify operations staff and the teachers who

New School Building Ribbon Cutting Ceremony, 2016

were available for the

coming school year. The first lesson we learned was to never hire from a place of desperation. At least four of six faculty members hired were individuals who were leaving their positions at DOE schools and expressed interest in working at a charter school after learning how it was different from a regular public school.

They were disgruntled and refused to comply with the accountability required in a high-expectations environment and more interested in creating confusion, engaging students inappropriately and carrying out an agenda that seemed to ride the tails of the DOE's targeted goal to destroy us before we got started. Instead of planning lessons they were planning disruption to the academic program. This toxic energy and the levels of insubordination became a day-to-day battleground.

Only six months after opening our doors, by February of 2007 there was a predictable, yet unexpected, outcome. I started receiving long memorandums from the faculty who were apparently meeting and drawing up plans to file a grievance for a long list of policies and practices that they did not like and wanted to change. Grievances is what unions were made of. As a charter school, we were not required to have one. The complaints ranged from not having enough prep or lunch time, being asked to cover classes when a colleague was absent, to the length of the school day, salaries, and finally, accusations that they were being harassed and intimidated by me. The communication of high expectations and accountability began to feel like a threat to the faculty who wanted to do the minimum without adhering to high expectations for performance. They were not at all interested in being a part of the mission to create a high-performing learning environment. They began to communicate with members of my board and circumvented the protocols for sharing concerns with me, as the head of school, first. The executive members of my board began expressing concerns about the conditions and the allegations that were being made by the faculty.

Several weeks later, it became clear that the staff's unprofessional conduct was a result of their being coached and enabled by the CSO at the DOE as well as the UFT who planted mediocre teachers to sabotage our charter school. Even though we were not a unionized school, I was able to discern that this approach was aligned with what some of my wiser and more seasoned colleagues described as an infiltration of destructive DOE union moles who were posing as faculty members, who were supposedly "dedicated" to the mission, values, and ideals at our charter school. In fact, it was just the opposite. They wanted to disrupt and shut down the school. The union has historically opposed charter schools and has always spread the narrative that we were out to destroy and replace the public school system and that we wanted to siphon money from the school districts to run our schools. Charter schools are public institutions and, in accordance with the NYS Charter law, the funding comes from the public school districts where the students are from. The per-pupil allocation is not equal to the amount of funding that the NYC public schools receive.

The union handprints were all over the scenario that was unfolding. The leaders at the CSO were right there actively colluding with the "gang of four" disgruntled staff, providing "technical assistance" and guidance about how to get the board's attention to have me brought up on charges and fired, which of course meant the immediate and premature death of the vision for equity in the Bronx. And it wasn't just our imagination that led us to believe this was going on behind the scenes. Years later, we were able to obtain documents and email through a Freedom of Information Law (FOIL) request that proved that this was not paranoia but an actual strategic plan that was developed during that time, using taxpayer-funded DOE's and NYSED's time and money to try to destroy the school.

THE PERFECT STORM

The tensions and political dynamics continued to build up to what became a perfect storm. The conflicts ranged from students who objected to the high behavioral expectations, the discipline and structure of a charter school, the length of the school day, and my no-nonsense, take-no-prisoners leadership style. The parents of some of these students were receiving constant negative communication and misinformation from some of the teachers. This barrage of lies manipulated their emotions and had them questioning their decision to place their child in a charter school.

It was later disclosed that the group of four disgruntled teachers who led the disruption of our new school initiative were communicating with the leaders at the charter school's office and sent their complaints to the Board of Trustees. This created a volatile attack and downward spiral followed by tumultuous board meetings that focused on what the response should be. The board leadership appeared to be more concerned about their reputations and their own personal conflicts of interests and ongoing political business dealings with the DOE than with the truth of the matter. The divisions that were intentionally created by the leadership at the CSO and the seeds of doubts that were planted by the gang of four were clearly not in my favor as the charter school's leader.

Perception was reality for many of those sitting on the board. These included a business manager of a bank who became the chair, the executive director for a nonprofit CBO who also operated a school, an attorney who supported numerous civil rights and social causes, and a local businessman. The board had an obligation to conduct their own investigation into the allegations that were being made about the charter school's operations, as well as the personal accusations against me as its leader. The board also had the ultimate responsibility of protecting the charter school from being closed and upholding their duty of loyalty to the bylaws of our organization.

They were clearly at the point of second-guessing their decision to support me as the school's leader. It was a lonely walk as the support had been lukewarm from the start, as a few members on the board did not really believe in the power of the vision that I had or were not familiar with charter schools. Some were ready to give in to the demands that the DOE was making, pushing them to force me to resign as the instructional leader, which would mean terminating my contract.

They did not fully comprehend the independence and autonomy that they had as a board or the fact that the DOE's leadership motives needed to be questioned. They did not want to see our charter school exist from the start. The same leaders in the CSO who colluded with the faculty plan to disrupt our educational environment were the same people who sabotaged our charter school application at every turn and step of the way. These behaviors were fueled by the UFT and condoned by the staff at the Office of Charter Schools at the DOE. What was really required was a close examination of the characters who were behind the strategy to shut us down within eight months of operations. As part of the strategy, I initially agreed to temporarily step down as principal and continue working on the development of the charter school's business and operations.

There was a protest and a student walkout that was being planned and led by the angry group of faculty members with the support of the UFT. After the protest outside of the school on May 11, 2007,

I received a call from the associate director of the Office of Charter Schools at the DOE, advising me that they were aware of the walkout and that the communications office for the chancellor would be issuing an official statement on behalf of the DOE and warned me not to speak to the press. She expressed concerns about the disruption of the academic program and warned that this had triggered an official visit and meeting. They now wanted the board to conduct its own investigation and meet with the teachers and students.

It became clear shortly thereafter that she and the then chief portfolio officer were boldly and shamefully in contact with this group of teachers and intimately aware of the strategy and their plan and providing support and encouragement. However, no one had the courtesy of contacting me to prepare me or give me a heads-up. Silence equals agreement and this was their form of payback for fighting for the right to exist and not allowing the haters to squash the dream for our charter school before we even got started.

I was in my office at the end of the day, and I was devastated. The world was tumbling down around me. My head was spinning and I finally had reached a breaking point. I was so distraught and began to sob uncontrollably. I knew that I was surrounded by a hostile and well-orchestrated attack. I was not dealing with a normal situation and could only trust my husband. The public assault and humiliation that I had experienced earlier that day and during the weeks leading up to that moment was beyond comprehension.

I just wanted to provide a quality education to the high school youth from the Bronx. The pressure became unbearable. What would happen to the students and families who enrolled at our charter school if we were crushed? I was almost ready to give up the fight when suddenly the path that should be taken became crystal clear. I had a revelation that brought all into focus. We were being set up to fail by the staff at the Charter Schools Office at the DOE and the NYSED. I advised the board that I wanted them to consider an independent investigation that would expose the truth behind what was really occurring, and if the findings corroborated that I had done anything illegal, immoral, or unethical, I would resign from my position and then the board could do what it wanted with the charter school.

The board agreed and hired Fulbright & Jaworski, one of the world's largest law firms, to conduct this investigation. I also retained an attorney to represent me as it was clear that I needed legal protection to protect my human rights, dignity, and self-respect.

I was not surprised that my dream for education equity in the Bronx was being trampled upon, forcing that we abandon establishing the charter school. However, I was still not ready to take no for an answer. They had all underestimated my tenacity and determination.

THE INDEPENDENT INVESTIGATION

The board agreed with the strategy to call for an independent investigation. In the letter the board points out that the DOE had prematurely launched its own investigation, thereby curtailing the board's legal governance responsibility to conduct its own. What follows is an excerpt of the letter from the International Leadership Board to Garth Harries, chief portfolio officer at the Charter Schools Office, and to Lisa Long, charter school staff at NYSED, in response to the allegations and outlining its plans to bring objective closure to the issues raised.

"...We recognize that the School faces serious challenges that require immediate action on our part. Indeed, we have already begun to take action. On May 7, 2007, we held an emergency meeting attended by the entire Board of Trustees, by the

School's legal counsel and by representatives of the New York City Center for Charter School Excellence. At that meeting, we took steps toward delivering a formal response to the allegations contained in the May 1, 2007 letter. We also adopted measures to ensure the stability of the academic program and of the School community, including a plan to dispatch members of the Board to the School to meet with concerned students, parents, teachers and staff. One such meeting—between members of the Board and several teachers and staff members—took place on May 9, 2007 and was positive and productive.

In addition to reaching out to the School community, we acknowledge the need for an investigation regarding the concerns expressed by you, by individual parents and by certain former teachers. To that end, we are in the process of retaining an independent law firm to conduct a comprehensive, independent investigation of the School and its Chief Executive Officer and Principal, Dr. Elaine Ruíz López – a decision Dr. López fully supports. Based on that investigation's findings, we will conduct an evaluation of the School and Dr. López, and we will deliver a formal, written response that addresses the concerns and grievances that have been brought to our attention. Please be assured that we will take all necessary and appropriate action to remedy any deficiencies that the investigation may uncover.

We welcome independent investigation to objectively assess the challenges we face, and we are confident that it will help us resolve the complaints that we have received. Pending the outcome of that investigation – and subject to its findings—we wish to take this opportunity to state the following in response to a number of the allegations set forth in the May 1, 2007 letter… "

After the board signed the contract engagement for the investigation that would cost the school $70,000, Fulbright & Jaworski were assigned to this investigation. I later learned the significance of having this particular attorney assigned to this case as our cause was one that was rooted in social justice and human rights. One of its top attorneys in the firm was Ralph C. Dawson, an African American who graduated from Columbia Law School in 1976, then Harvard and Yale. I learned years later in my research that his background included his role as the leader of the Black Student Alliance at Yale (BSAY) during the tumultuous period known as "May Day 1970," when New Haven, Connecticut, and Yale were the site of a major murder trial involving the Black Panther Party and a series of protests against the Vietnam War. The BSAY played a crucial role in keeping the peace on the campus, generating support for the conduct of a fair trial for the Black Panthers.[60]

Mr. Dawson deposed approximately twenty-five individuals during the investigation. Most of the interviews were conducted at our school site. He was professional and appeared to be objective. I felt comfortable with the process and was confident that he would not find anything that was illegal, immoral, or unethical in the way I made decisions in accordance with policy, supervised staff, and actions taken in my role as the school leader. The outcome to this investigation would impact the future of our charter school and whether I would continue as its lead. After approximately six weeks, the investigation was over. I waited anxiously for the written report and outcome as

---

60   The Sophia Institute, 2020.

this would be an important factor in the strategy to save the charter school and putting all of the facts on the table.

ROBIN CALITRI

Mr. Calitri was a former principal of a highly successful IB school in Rockville, Long Island. Robin was named The New York State Distinguished Educator in 1998[61] and one of four finalists for the National Association of Secondary School Principals' Principal of the Year in 1999. Mr. Calitri has shared his acumen with thousands of educators, parents, and children by way of presentations, articles, and workshops—all focused on the concept that "All Means All." Robin represented the International Baccalaureate (IB) organization and served as a member of The Development team for Re-Engineering Schools. He also served as a commissioner for the publication of "Breaking Ranks II"[62] by the National Association of Secondary School Principals and is a *Certified Breaking Ranks II Trainer*. The International Baccalaureate Organization enlisted Robin to be the school designer for a small new school's project in New York City.

Working as a member of a team, he helped develop the International Leadership Charter School in the Bronx. I was introduced to Robin by Tony, who at the time was working with Civic Strategies, a school improvement organization that he was a consultant for.

While I was in the process of developing the charter school application, I learned of his work in Rockville and found out that he was an expert in school leadership, high school curriculum development,

---

61 Previous State Principals of the Year, https://www.nassp.org/previous-state-principals-of-the-year/.

62 Vicki Kilgarriff, Breaking Ranks II: Strategies for Leading High School Reform. National Association of Secondary School Principals. Forward by Theodore R. Sizer. 2004.

and had the formula for building a successful college prep sequence. I realized I needed him as part of the planning team. I hired him as a consultant to assist me in thinking through and developing the school's academic program and college prep sequence, a component to our instructional model that is successful to this date, even eighteen years later. I am sure that Robin never imagined that one year later I would ask him to become coprincipal after the smoke settled and we were able to stabilize our academic program. I will be eternally grateful to Robin as there was no one else that could be trusted in that climate.

For my own protection, as well as what was left of my sanity and dignity, I proposed to the board that I would voluntarily remove myself from those day-to-day supervisory duties as principal, pending the outcome of the investigation(s). The board agreed to this approach. This required support with the supervision of faculty and the instructional program. In addition, there were substitute teachers who were retained after the faculty who disrupted our learning environment were terminated. I reassured them that this would only be for a few months until the investigation was over. I needed support with the supervision of faculty and the immediate restoration of the academic program and student discipline. This was an important strategy to win the battle that I found myself mired in. I hired two former school principals and administrators, Robin Calitri and Carmen Gonzalez. Carmen started working for the school as a staff developer and content area expert for the science program. While writing this chapter, I reconnected with Robin and asked him to reflect on his work at the time, and what was being asked of him. In his own words he writes:

"I left the New York City Public Schools in eighth grade. A counselor had informed me that I had no future in academics and that I ought to attend the school of printing trades in lieu of high school. I vowed then that I would never enter a NYC

school because of the im-personalization, low expectations and dehumanizing of students. Acting as an evaluator of a NYC high school for the state and attending training for the New Small Schools Project reinforced my disillusionment. Fifty or so years later, I found myself addressing 350 NYC principals and other administrators about my belief that "All Means All". I was also advising one of the premier NYC high schools and had been named as school designer for potential public International Baccalaureate schools in NYC. The biggest surprise was when I accepted the challenge to become acting principal for a newborn charter school under attack.

I was involved in the initial formation of the International Leadership Charter School as a staff trainer and consultant. I was impressed at the zeal of the founder, Dr. Elaine Ruíz López, the Board of Directors, and some of the staff. In the latter part of the first school year, the school and the founder were seemingly under attack. The assaults came from the teachers' union, the State Education Department, the office of charter schools staff at the DOE and some local civic leaders. The demand was that Dr. Ruíz López remove herself from the administration of the school or the school would cease to exist. Elaine pleaded with us to lead the school so that she can have time to regroup and to save the school year. Carmen Gonzalez, a retired school principal, who was working as a coach and staff developer was also asked to step in. We agreed to co-lead the school for the last two months of the school year. We were simply part of a team which was focused on the well-being of the 9th graders attending the International Leadership Charter High School, so we went to work.

The external pressure caused some teachers to quit. We filled in with under-qualified substitutes. We refined goals to focus on the NYS Algebra Regents exam since passage on that exam is the only externally moderated measure of 'what kids know and are able to do' in ninth grade. We revised the curriculum, struggled with discipline, and fought the external hordes. We just did it and the kids came through! The fledgling charter school outperformed the competition. We had positioned ourselves to compare results with other local, public schools whose results were typically dismal. I continued to consult with the school for a few years and watched with joy as it continued to succeed and its charges flourish.

I have used this school as an example of how to make schools work. A safe environment is crucial. Good curriculum and instruction is key. Uniforms, discipline, and respect for one another among the students are valuable. Leadership is crucial. What makes schools work for kids is that the students are cherished and cared for.

The International Leadership Charter High School, under the stewardship of Dr. Elaine Ruíz López, is a raving success because it has been nurtured, molded, and fiercely protected by a team of wonderful people. They have chosen a model of schooling and are establishing a future for some wonderful children who may not always have access to an excellent education due to the structural inequities in our society, prejudices, and the miasma of politics in our educational system. I am proud to have played my small part."

On the evening of the May 5, 2007 walkout, I was alone in the building with Robin, who advised me that there were two investigators at the door who were requesting access to personnel files. They were two white males dressed in black who showed up to the school at 5 p.m. Were they detectives? FBI? They did not immediately identify themselves and we were not sure who they were or what office they represented as they were very cloak-and-dagger in their introduction.

Upon presenting a business card we allowed them into my office. They were investigators from the Special Commissioner Investigations (SCI)—an agency that is independent from the NYCDOE with oversight authority. SCI investigates misappropriation of funds, sexual abuse of students, conflicts of interest, corruption and fraud, and any other criminal activity that hinders the education of children in the NYC public school system.

Although we were technically authorized by the Chancellor's Office of Charter Schools, we were not part of the public school system. I learned that as a charter school we were not obligated to turn over these files without an official subpoena, which they did not have. I informed them that they could not take the files but that we would make copies of the pertinent items in the files to cooperate. Could matters get worse? Was I being accused of something nefarious? Or was this just more harassment? They did not request my personnel files, which was a bit of a relief. Oddly, they seemed to be focused on the teachers who demonstrated outside of our school earlier that morning. So now it appeared that there were two investigations that were taking place. The independent investigation by Fulbright & Jaworski and one being conducted by SCI. Why was there suddenly going to be an investigation by this office?

CHAPTER 15

LOSING THE BATTLE
TO WIN THE WAR

> "No temptation has overtaken you except what
> is common to mankind. And God is faithful; he
> will not let you be tempted beyond what you
> can bear. But when you are tempted, he will also
> provide a way out so that you can endure it."
> —I CORINTHIANS 10:13

The Fulbright & Jaworski investigation was conclusive—
no illegal, immoral, or unethical activities were discovered. I had fulfilled my duties as the school's principal
and CEO, protecting student safety and implementing
the school's charter. There were no celebrations upon receiving this
news, except for a few lukewarm congratulations; it was more a relief
than a victory.

THE INVESTIGATION FINDINGS

In the Fulbright & Jaworski L.L.P. report[63] to the Board of Directors of the International Leadership Charter School, the lead attorney for the Fulbright investigation, Ralph Dawson, conducted interviews of twenty-five persons including several in-person and by phone interviews with me to obtain my position on various issues and to facilitate review of relevant facts, and also interviewed individuals at other organizations who had relevant information. Fulbright also reviewed personnel files with respect to several of the teachers, the International Leadership Charter School's bylaws, personnel manual, parent student handbook, and charter. Fulbright also reviewed files concerning certain students and incidents that appear to be significant from our interviews with the various persons; we also reviewed documents and other information obtained in the interviews and from other relevant sources based upon the interviews conducted and review of the documents provided by the International Leadership Charter School and from other sources.

In the final report, Fulbright has concluded that:

"Dr. López had a reasonable basis for actions with respect to most of the complaints and complied with most procedural requirements. It appears that Dr. López had grounds to discharge specific faculty members and that she also had bases for either reprimanding or guiding other teachers and that the discipline almost always was not well received and contributed to the circumstances that resulted in disruptions at the school confrontations and distress among some parents... and led to the events which contributed to disruptions in the school

---

63   The Report of Fulbright and Jaworksi L.L.P. to the Board of Directors of International Leadership Charter School. July 1, 2007.

environment. Notwithstanding the disruptions, International Leadership Charter School appears to have provided a good educational experience to its students. The report further found that there was no evidence that the International Leadership Charter School administration took actions to prevent teachers from engaging in union organization."

The Fulbright report also concludes:

"Viewing the foregoing circumstances, we believe that Dr. López had reason to be concerned about whether to renew the contracts of the four teachers who resigned in May of 2007. The teachers felt that Dr. López was too strict in the way she attempted to enforce the rules. However, the memorandum from the teacher evince events that they were stern and aggressive in their dealings with Dr. López as well. The investigator further concludes that the teachers made so many requests in April 2007 and did so in a fashion which appeared calculated, to overwhelm Dr. López' administrative attention… many of the requests were not necessarily for information to which they were entitled for example a written explanation of the rationale for beginning classroom observations at this point in the school year a list of all trustees their positions on the board and their contact information and prior notice of the expected time of scheduled visits to the classroom by outside visitors and April 25th memorandum essentially questions whether Dr. López can [enforce professional attire]…moreover the tone of the memorandum were confrontational and somewhat disrespected disrespectful including one inquiring about the status of MetroCard stating we've been patient but we expect you to resolve this issue immediately and to address reimbursement costs for this week's transportation

further they were trying to force Dr. López to deal with them collectively which she had no obligation to do. Parents felt equally strongly that Dr. López is pivotal to achieving the vision of the school which they view as a school with a strong code of conduct which provides a structured school environment which will instill the focus and discipline they believe their children need to succeed…there is good news in the situation however since there are parents on both sides of the dispute who appear to have a genuine interest in the success of the school and Dr. López also committed to the success of the school."

The insubordination, outrageous behaviors, and disruption to the education of our students by this small group of faculty was intentional. These behaviors were fueled and emboldened by external parties who viewed charter schools as a threat to the status quo. The UFT has historically viewed charter schools as a threat to the status quo and supported this calculated attack. Unfortunately, we had hired individuals who were not the right fit for the first year of a new charter school. This behavior resulted in significant disruptions to our educational programs. Despite having to start over with new faculty who were primarily substitutes, in the aftermath of a faculty protest and student walkout in May, I continued to strategize with Robin Calitri and Carmen Gonzalez and remained focused on the preparation of our students for the upcoming June NYS Regents exams while an investigation was taking place.

With the support of colleagues and the Center for Educational Partnerships we were able to identify proctors and a scoring team for the administration of the NYS Regents exam in Algebra and Living Environment. I did not know what to expect as there were so many distractions and interruptions to teaching and learning. At the June board meeting the outcome of the investigation was discussed and documented into the minutes. The reception to the news was anti-climactic. I was relieved and although it was certainly something to celebrate, I did not feel a party was necessary. I was exonerated and it was no longer the plan for me to resign and step down from my role. As I resumed my duties as the CEO and school leader, I felt vindicated and was very grateful that the board agreed to the investigation.

STUDENT PERFORMANCE

Despite these disruptions, the student performance on the NYS Regents exam was commendable, with 66 percent passing the Living Environment exam and 67 percent passing the Algebra Exam. Though below our usual standards, given the orchestrated disruption it was a respectable outcome, showcasing the effectiveness of our instruction even amid challenges. However, it was only the end of the first year, just after the school was turned on its head. One board member acknowledged that our school performed higher than most NYC public high schools and that it was evident that despite the circumstances, effective instruction was taking place. Several months later, when the official record and NYC and NYS report cards were released, it was clear that we had outperformed the neighboring high schools in the Bronx.

I received lukewarm congratulatory comments from the board members, and it appeared that some were surprised at the favorable outcome on both the scores and the independent investigation. There was indeed light at the end of a dark tunnel, and these results, along with the well-documented findings and conclusions made by Ralph C. Dawson, the lead attorney in the investigation, shifted the outlook and future of our charter school. It was a pivotal moment among many more moments that still were ahead of us. More than half of the board members present at this final meeting would eventually realize that it was time for them to move on as board members, and one by one they tendered their resignations.

The SCI typically investigates cases of child physical and sexual abuse, sexual misconduct, corruption, fraud, and fiscal malfeasance within the NYCDOE. The results of the SCI investigation were centered on one teacher, who I later learned had been fired from the New York City public schools for misconduct. The personnel division at DOE was not sharing its Do Not Hire (DNH) list and there was no way of knowing if the teachers who were being interviewed had a record of misconduct. Apparently, when the news coverage of the walkout was on all the media, there were photographs showing this teacher and identifying her by name. She had been dismissed for inappropriate behavior at the high school where she had been previously employed. It was serious enough that the DOE fired her and unfortunately, we had mistakenly hired her without knowing her background, and thereby inherited the problem.

When I was called down to the SCI to give testimony, I was accompanied to 80 Maiden Lane by Jesse Berman, a prominent and progressive criminal defense attorney whom I retained at the recommendation of Marianita Lopez, an attorney and New York University Law School graduate who was also Tony's aunt. Mr. Berman advised me to cooperate and to simply stick to the facts and the questions that I was being asked. It was an insane situation, and the intimidation was so great that I could not trust going alone. Oddly, most of the questions were about a few of the faculty who led the disruption and were focused on the hiring process that I engaged in, including whether resumes were submitted, applications completed, references checked, and who made the final decision for hiring.

There was also a great deal of curiosity about how I was initially contacted by one of the four teachers who led the walkout. It appears that this individual was terminated from the NYCDOE a few years before our school's opening; however, she was never officially prosecuted for the crime allegedly committed against a student. This meant that there were no flags on the fingerprints to prevent any school outside of the DOE from hiring this individual. After the investigation was completed, there was no report shared or published. There was a letter issued to my board in 2007 advising us to review our charter school's hiring practices with little to no significant conclusion, impact, or implications. After about two years the information regarding the allegations made about this teacher and the termination from the DOE mysteriously vanished from the archives on the SCI website.

"¡PA'LANTE!" (ONWARD!)

It was the fall of 2007, and the dust had settled temporarily. I had to prepare the team for a new cohort of students who were registered and were starting in the fall. We had to hire faculty for the tenth grade. We needed to move forward and resume day-to-day operations. Using lessons learned from our previous years of experience, we were careful to hire trustworthy individuals who showed loyalty to our vision. In addition, we had to rebuild the board as we picked up the pieces from the damage intentionally caused by those who were on the DOE payroll. They lacked integrity, thrived on chaos, destroying dreams, and tearing down leaders of color by creating mistrust, colluding with personal attacks and public humiliation, and planting seeds of doubt in the charter school's ability to succeed. I desperately needed to hire an instructional leader who would be willing to learn and support the charter school's vision and take the risk of signing onto a school that had a target on its back and on probation.

I hired Ms. Roberta Cummings whose previous experience was as principal of a Greek religious independent school. I liked her immediately. She was tall, elegant, and had a stern, no-nonsense demeanor. Ms. Cummings is of Jamaican heritage and impressed me as someone who would take leadership, challenge me without feeling intimidated by my role, and an unapologetic approach to leadership—a necessary battle tool to survive the attacks that our school was constantly facing. She was God-sent and the leader that I needed to stay grounded and to maintain the integrity of the academic program while I strategized and focused on having the charter school removed from probation. During the writing of this manuscript, I reached out to Roberta and asked her to reflect on her experience and work with me.

A NAPKIN, A PLANE, AND HIGH EXPECTATIONS—ROBERTA CUMMINGS

"When I started in the role as Director of Curriculum and Instruction at the International Leadership Charter High School in July of 2007, I was absolutely elated and excited at the idea of working at a newly founded charter school in its second year of operation. I vividly remember my interview with Dr. Elaine Ruíz López who was the Founder and CEO of the school. I waited anxiously in the main lobby and observed the bustling office staff who communicated and interacted with each other with a high-level of professionalism. I was impressed and wanted to be a part of the team. Shortly after, Dr. López came out and greeted me with a warm smile and a firm handshake. "Hi, Ms. Cummings, welcome to the International Leadership Charter High School."

The first week in my role consisted of reading the Charter, the renewal visit report, and other curriculum documents as part of my on-boarding process. At the time, my office space was adjacent and located outside of Dr. López's office. While reading the renewal visit report, I began to realize that the school (at the time) was placed on "probation." Honestly, I thought to myself, what did I sign up for? My first week also consisted of meetings with Dr. López, who was remarkably transparent about some of the challenges ILCHS was facing and also shared insights regarding the political obstacles Charter schools often face in their attempt provide a world-class education for black and brown scholars, while also providing families with choice. One of my other tasks as the new DCI was to assist Dr. López with hiring a new cadre of teachers for our

Roberta Cummings and Dr. López

sophomore cohort. I learned many valuable things under the guidance of Dr. López during my tenure at ILCHS, however one of the most critical things I learned, was the importance of hiring world-class teachers even if that meant recruiting talent out of state or even out of the country. The hiring agency that we used at the time had a pool of highly educated and experienced educators. Dr. López was passionate about hiring the best to help us "build the plane as we were flying it" which was one her many mantras. I learned many mantras from Dr. López during our many check-in meetings that still prove valuable in my work today in schools with students and staff. Another mantra was "No one rises to low expectations." This particular mantra is one that I have held on to firmly because I believe it helped me to ground and stay focus on the work and mission we were trying to achieve at ILCHS. Despite the challenges that came with "building the plane as we were flying it," I consistently observed the resiliency, and resoluteness of Dr. López, whose goal was always to ensure that scholars were able to meet and exceed expectations. In one of my later check-in meetings, Dr. López shared her vision and how ILCHS begun. At the time I was expecting her to share that it was a lifelong dream that was fully thought out and developed. Rather what she shared was the opposite; she wrote the dream and plan of starting a charter school on a napkin. I thought to myself, a napkin? Fast forward 16 years later the inspiration that started on a napkin has grown into a high-performing school that has allowed hundreds of black and brown children to graduate and begin successful college and career pathways, a manifestation that one can only rise to high expectations."

To maintain effective governance, we had to carefully examine each board applicant for the required skill sets that included strong character and integrity, and who would operate independently and maintain a duty of loyalty to the charter schools' bylaws and trust, as well as the school leaders' decisions and insights. This also required independent thinkers from outside of the public school system, who were socially and politically conscious, believed in the mission and vision of the charter school, and especially in our right to exist. It would take another two years before we had a board who fully supported our vision and would intentionally resist and challenge the whims and threats coming from the staff at the DOE. We strategically recruited from the best, tapping on our closest colleagues and professional network to start with a clean slate and build a board that could function as an autonomous entity, focused on maintaining oversight of the fiscal, organizational, and academic aspects of the charter school. It was an ongoing struggle and we had to lose a few battles to eventually win the war.

Throughout the next three years, the staff at the DOE and NYSED continued to interfere. They made frequent attempts to over-scrutinize our policies, academic program, and operational activities in the name of "compliance." It would take at least another four years until our first charter renewal to operate without drama and to shift the mindset of all stakeholders to support a school that had extraordinary potential to succeed, as opposed to one that had a target on it as dead on arrival (DOA).

The primary obstacles to our success as a charter school continued to be the bad actors who were overpaid with public dollars, to engage in highly unprincipled actions at the DOE in collaboration with the NYSED. It appeared that there was enough evidence through a FOIL request that was initiated by Kerry Flowers, an attorney who was a close colleague and friend of our board chair John Paul Gonzalez, that proved that senior staff at these two offices had colluded together and were determined to destabilize our school community and to have our charter revoked. They were unsuccessful on the first attempt; however, they were not done. We were placed on probation in the fall of 2007 with a list of conditions that had to be put in place. Although we complied with most of the conditions within less than a year, the leadership at the charter school's office refused to put in writing that we had complied with all terms and conditions. We were not removed from this probationary status until 2010, after a long-term battle when we escalated to the former Chancellor Joel Klein and members of the NYS Board of Regents.

The CSO at the DOE were obsessed and single-minded about shutting down a school that promised a world of opportunity for education equity in the Bronx for thousands of first-generation immigrant students before it had an opportunity to thrive and grow. It was hard not to take these actions personally. I couldn't help but wonder if these aggressions would have existed if I had been a white woman of privilege with the backing of foundation money.

We chose to continue to fight to protect our charter school and to have the DOE remove us from this death sentence. We could not let our guard down and we needed legal support. We pursued representation and received pro bono support from a prominent law firm in lower Manhattan, Hughes Hubbard & Reed (HHR). On November 1, 2007, the law firm of HHR hand-delivered a letter to Garth Harries, executive director of the Office of Portfolio Development, NYCDOE, regarding the matter concerning International Leadership Charter High School's probationary status. Eduardo Vidal, lead counsel, addresses a letter addressed to the school board of trustees, October 12, 2007. Mr. Vidal writes:

> *"You stated that the DOE was extending the probationary period of the school until the close of the 2007-2008 academic year with the right to summarily revoke the school charter effective July 1st 2008 if the school failed to comply with revised probationary terms. The school was originally placed on probation May 14th, 2007, for the remainder of the 2006-2007 academic school year pending further investigation based on a number of incidents that occurred during the academic year. Pursuant to this initial probationary order the DOE recommended a corrective action plan for the school to implement in order to remedy these problems. On June 5th 2007 the DOE conducted an on-site assessment of the school's*

educational program to determine the extent which the school had implemented its corrective action plan based on the findings of this visit it was concluded that the school had not satisfied the terms of the correction corrective action plan. Despite numerous requests by Dr. Elaine Ruíz López neither the school authorities nor the board of trustees have received a copy of the report that was used by the DOE to place the school on probation. In the absence of providing a copy of this report the DOE cannot fairly ask the school to hit a moving target."

In Mr. Vidal's concluding statement he writes:

"Finally we recognize that under article 52 section 2885 (2) of New York's education law the DOE has the power to revoke the charter of the school however section 2885 (2) is also very clear that prior to the revocation of a school's charter the school must be afforded due process which in our view would encompass fair consideration of all the facts available in the very least the DOE needs to take into consideration and incorporate whatever rebuttals or clarifications the school presents into the findings it issues furthermore we respectfully request that in the event that the DOE disagrees with any information offered by school authorities the reasons behind such a decision be disclosed in writing."

I continued to focus on stabilizing the academic program and the selective hiring of highly qualified teachers dedicated to the achievement of our students. The first cohort of students was greatly impacted and confused by the actions taken by their former teachers, who had used them for their own personal agendas and selfish motives. By nature, adolescents are suspicious of adults and rebellious to authority. They continued to be resistant to the discipline and structure that was expected of them, but we refused to give up on them and sought to restore their trust.

In 2010 the first cohort of the fifty-four students who maintained enrollment status would become the first graduating class, and ninety-nine percent of those who were continuously enrolled graduated. Today, eighteen years later we have graduated thirteen cohorts of high school students, all of whom were accepted to the college of their choice. More than 85 percent every year have enrolled into mostly four-year colleges and have pursued their field of study in Engineering, Computer Science, Business, Criminal Justice, Education, Law, Counseling, and Social Work. Hundreds of students from cohorts I to IX (class of 2010 through class of 2019) have now graduated from college.

SUPPORT GROWS

During this same period in 2009, leaders in the Puerto Rican/Latino community started to notice the injustice our school was subjected to. They actively supported my leadership in the charter school arena and began to seek me out for consults on their own desire and dream to open charter schools. The most fascinating of them all was when I heard from my childhood pediatrician, Dr. Richard Izquierdo.

BUILDING INSTITUTIONS AND LEGACY

Dr. Richard Izquierdo—affectionately known as "Doc"—was born in East Harlem on October 23, 1929. His parents Serafin and Sinda Izquierdo were Puerto Ricans and were part of the original "*bodegue-ros.*" Doc's dedication has always been to serve the medical needs of his community. For many years, he was one of the few doctors in the community. He became an icon for the South Bronx neighborhood and was the "*el doctor*" sought out by Puerto Ricans in the area.

In 1967, Doc purchased an abandoned building on Southern Boulevard and Westchester Avenue with a down payment of $3,000 to create the San Juan Health Center. It operated until 1974, when it became the Urban Health Plan (UHP), Inc., a federally qualified community health center licensed by New York State. His daughter Paloma Hernandez is the CEO for UHP that provides comprehensive quality healthcare to the community. Today, UHP is one of the largest health centers in New York State. On January 23, 2007, Doc was awarded the Surgeon General's Medallion from the 17th Surgeon General of the United States, Richard H. Carmona, MD. This award is the highest honor that the Surgeon General can bestow on a civilian or officer. Doc was Dr. Carmona's pediatrician and his lifelong personal mentor, and the childhood doctor for US Justice Sonia Sotomayor who was raised in the South Bronx. In fact, he was my pediatrician as well and one of his babies.

Dr. Richard Izquierdo with daughter, Paloma Hernandez, and US Supreme Court Justice Sonya Sotomayor

In 1998, I was at a social gathering in a local restaurant, and I heard that Dr. Izquierdo was in the room. I was immediately drawn to where he was standing, and I introduced myself to him and politely interrupted the intimate group of people that he was speaking with. I introduced myself and informed him that he was my pediatrician, and that I was one of his "babies." He smiled broadly, deep blue eyes twinkling. He was very welcoming and gracious.

I had only a limited amount of time with this very well-respected man who was loved by many. In about five minutes I rattled off who I was, that I had graduated from TC, received my doctorate from Columbia University, and that I was working on a plan to start a school in the Bronx and was committed to doing something great in the community like he had done. He spoke to me about the UHP and the work that was being done there.[64] We exchanged contact information, although it would be eight years before we would reconnect again. After establishing UHP with his daughter he did not stop dreaming and planning initiatives to improve the community. One of Doc's final initiatives before he passed away in July of 2020 was his dream to provide a quality education to free the children of the South Bronx from the bonds of poverty.

After that meeting, we temporarily lost contact with one another. However, in 2008, Doc learned more about me and the charter high school that we had opened two years earlier through a colleague. He contacted me, informing me that he wanted to start a charter school and requested a meeting. One afternoon in the fall of 2009, he visited me at our charter school. I reminded him again that we had previously met and that he was my childhood pediatrician. He asked me to describe my parents and he told me that he remembered Lucila.

After he shared his vision with me, he asked me if I could help him with his dream and provide guidance. I was running my own charter school and my time was limited; however, I could not pass up the opportunity to support this iconic figure who was respected by so many and whom I had such fond memories of. We met a few times at the UHP and at our school, and I shared the documents that we had submitted for our application with him. In September 2010, his dream was fulfilled with the opening of the Dr. Richard Izquierdo

---

64   Urban Health Plan, https://www.urbanhealthplan.org/our-community/.

Health and Science Charter School (DRHSCS) on 800 Home Street in the South Bronx. The school was the first charter school in New York City to offer a Career and Technical Education program geared specifically toward preparing students for jobs in the healthcare sector, including the Emergency Medical Technician (EMT) certification.

By 2012, the charter school was struggling due to internal politics and staff who were not mission aligned. Tony was asked by Doc to help him stabilize the school's academic program and operations. In 2014, we attended the first graduation. The school is still thriving today and operating out of the same DOE school building. Tony and I felt honored to support his dream and delighted that he was able to fulfill his vision. In 2015, the very street located at Southern Boulevard and West Farms Avenue, where he started the San Juan Health Center, was renamed Dr. Richard Izquierdo Blvd.

Doc passed in July of 2020 from complications of Parkinson's disease. The impact of his contribution to the South Bronx and legacy will continue to benefit children and families through future generations.

CHAPTER 16

EXPANDING OUR IMPACT

> "Oh, that you would bless me and enlarge my territory!"
> **—I CHRONICLES 4:10**

Five years after starting our operations, our community charter school saw rising student achievements and immense support from parents and community leaders. We were experiencing growth in both enrollment and demand. My primary focus as an experienced educator was on the academic program, student safety, and their well-being.

Managing a charter school demands entrepreneurial skills, especially in understanding business nuances, vendor relationships, contracts, finances, and infrastructure. The facility we rented in 2006 began draining our finances, and dealing with a difficult landlord became a constant challenge. It became clear we needed to relocate. This urgency intensified when our landlord tried to evict us in 2010, putting the school's future in jeopardy.

Despite investing in renovating the facility into a state-of-the-art school, our relationship with the landlord deteriorated. He would often intrude without notice and bring potential clients to display the space, seemingly to intimidate. In-person meetings with him were tense, especially with his Doberman present. Safety concerns arose when on one occasion, cars in the building's garage, which he owned, caught fire. While he insisted we evacuate, FDNY officials advised against it, deeming it safer to stay indoors. Such incidents reinforced our need to find a new location, as it was evident the landlord prioritized his profits over the school's welfare.

> Five years after the shock of the first two years of operations and our trial by fire, our school was increasing its visibility as a community-grown charter school that had a steady upward increase in student achievement scores and an upswell of support from parents, community leaders, and our colleagues. We were growing in enrollment and demand. I was an experienced educator, and my focus had always been centered on the academic program, teaching, learning, and the safety and wellness of our scholars.
>
> My response was to remind him that we were a public school with a restricted budget and that we could not shake the money tree to install a new system that would have cost over $60,000. In the Spring we had to improvise and import fans for cooling and in the winter, we purchased heaters to keep the classrooms warm.

All charter school operators require an entrepreneurial spirit and willingness to be thrown into the deep end of the pool, to learn the world of business, vendor relationships, contracts, and finances, and, when seeking to expand, facilities and construction. The commercial facility that we leased in 2006 on Exterior Street in front of the Marble

Hill Houses to commence our operations in 2006 started to strangle our finances. It also divided my attention as the head of school, as I had to constantly manage a very difficult landlord. All the signs were present that it was time to move. It was evident that I desperately needed to identify financing to secure a permanent home where we could operate independently, and not be under pressure from the landlord who had attempted to evict us in 2010. This would have meant the collapse of the school and closure as we had no place to go, and the DOE was not going to provide colocation. They would have us right back in the position we were struggling with in 2007.

The landlord was charging us an extraordinarily high above-market rent, adding charges for items that were actually his responsibility to pay for. There was a rider in the lease that would trigger the payment of over $100,000 and we were having cashflow issues. This was a lease in a commercial facility that had many challenges, including poor heat in the winters and sweltering indoor temperatures in late spring, due to an outdated HVAC system in need of frequent repair and servicing. He needed constant reminders that we were a public school with a restricted budget and that we could not shake the money tree to install a new system that would have cost over $60,000. In the spring we had to improvise and import fans for cooling, and in the winter we purchased heaters to keep the classrooms warm. Despite these poor conditions, we paid rent on time of approximately $650,000 annually over five years, adding to his wealth.

We were shocked that he found a judge to sign an eviction notice to displace our entire school and our students. This meant that we could not continue operating past another charter term in 2015 and that we would have to find another location in a few months. Fortunately, my prayers for another miracle were answered and we received a check from an angel who showed up to our doorstep. Raul Russi, the former CEO of the Acacia network, had heard of our crisis through a colleague and brought us a check for $150,000 with no strings attached. I am eternally grateful to Acacia and Mr. Russi for their kind gesture. This was God at work. We were able to pay the bill to the landlord and avoid an eviction. For this, our parents and school community are eternally grateful.

One of my favorite quotes is *"Leap and the net will appear."* As a woman of faith, I prayed for support in renewing our charter in 2011. I received an invitation from the EDC under Mayor Bloomberg to apply for municipal bond financing. After much preparation and hiring a finance-savvy project associate, we were approved to seek underwriters for bonds to fund our school building. Despite the rigorous process and negotiations with Wall Street investors, we secured a bond of $17.5 million in the spring of 2013.

Operating a charter school meant becoming a businessperson overnight, requiring adaptability in finance and negotiations. Seeing other charter schools succeed, I was determined to achieve our goal. The prospect of owning our school building was enticing. After financing, we faced challenges in construction, from hiring contractors to delays in completion. However, by late 2015, with the intervention of the Borough President Ruben Diaz, Jr.'s Office, inspections were expedited. On January 1, 2016, we occupied our three-story school on Riverdale Avenue. Designed as envisioned, it featured science labs, a cafeteria, eighteen classrooms, and more, all adorned in our school colors. This was a dream realized for the future leaders of University Heights, Kingsbridge/Riverdale, and Marble Hill neighborhoods in District 10. I had somehow, through so much opposition and turmoil, been able to make this dream a reality!

CHAPTER 17

THE GROWTH OF A VISION: ONE DECADE LATER

> "I would hope that a wise Latina woman with the richness of her experiences would more often than not reach a better conclusion, than a white male who hasn't lived that life."
> **—US SUPREME COURT JUSTICE SONIA SOTOMAYOR**

We celebrated our tenth year anniversary in November of 2016 at a beautiful venue found nestled in the Bronx Botanical Gardens. All of our board chairs were in attendance along with parents, students, and colleagues. On this occasion, we honored NYS Board Regent Dr. Betty A. Rosa and Ms. Marlene Cintron, JD—two very strong Puerto Rican women who worked in various leadership positions in governmental politics and education, each holding sig-

From left to right: Dr. Dori Collazo-Baker, Dr. John Paul Gonzalez, Dr. Elaine Ruíz López, Anthony López, Dr. John Jenkins, Mrs. Jenkins, Doreen Bermudez, Elissa Ramos, and my father Alfonso Ruiz.

nificant roles in public service. I have admired both amazing leaders and considered them exemplary role models and mentors for over two decades. Today, Dr. Rosa is the New York State Commissioner of Education and President of the University of the State of New York. Dr. Rosa and I met when she was superintendent of District 8 in the late 1990s. She hired me as the assistant principal for an embattled elementary school in the Bronx that required strong leadership support for its principal.

Marlene Cintron and I

Ms. Cintron has worked for Congressman Garcia, Mayor Dinkins, Governor Rosello of Puerto Rico, and New York State Senator Ruben Diaz, Sr. and served the former Borough President Ruben Diaz, Jr. for eight years. In 2010, she was named president of the Bronx Overall Economic Development Corporation. Today, Marlene Cintron oversees SBA programs, offices, and operations in the SBA's Atlantic region, serving New York, New Jersey, Puerto Rico, and the US Virgin Islands. She supported me when the charter school and its development was just an idea. The support and wisdom from these two extraordinary women have contributed to my success as a leader of our charter school in its first decade and beyond.

I met my friend and colleague Dr. John Jenkins in 1999 while working as assistant principals in the Yonkers Public School (YPS) district. We served in this role under Dr. Fred Hernandez's leadership, who took on the challenge to turn around Roosevelt High School—a failing high school. This was amid a racially hostile environment and a court battle to force YPS to desegregate its schools.[65] John and I stayed in touch as colleagues, and he later became the board chair to support me and our charter school when it was still very fragile from the attempts to destabilize our school. Dr. Jenkins served from 2008 to 2012, and with his unwavering leadership as chair and his ability to call out the nefarious motives that he observed from senior staff working at the DOE's charter school's office, we were able to power through our very first five-year charter renewal.

In his reflection of his contribution and role in the development of International Leadership, Dr. Jenkins writes:

> *"When I first met Elaine, we were colleagues on the leadership team of a high school that was in need of improvement in the Yonkers Public School district. We were faced with consistent challenges, as well as political and racial opposition as we tried to create change on the behalf of a school population that contained a significant number of Black and Brown students. The school district was the last to fully honor the desegregation laws in the Northeast. Many referred to Yonkers PS district as "up south". It was in that context that I first realized that*

---

65   U.S. v. City of Yonkers, https://casetext.com/case/us-v-city-of-yonkers-2.

Elaine was a unique leader who had the vision, courage and commitment to do whatever it took to advocate on behalf of students and families that were not given the opportunity to advocate for themselves. It was that same confidence, courage and commitment that lived at the center of the mission and vision of the International Leadership Charter High School (International Leadership CHS). I remember one epiphanic moment when we were preparing our first defense of the initial proposal for the school at Tweed, the central office of the NYC DOE. While we were standing in a group waiting to be called in, a plastic bottle of water fell from somewhere high above and landed on Elaine's head. Although Elaine was stunned and taken aback by the impact, she was fortunately not seriously injured. Once Elaine gathered her composure and felt she was ok, she immediately shifted the concern group her supportive committee members back to the matter at hand and we began our journey toward defending the creation of the charter school. I feel as if that moment, it was a foreshadowing of the litany of attacks to come. Like the bottle, they often seemed to fall from nowhere at key opportune moments in our journey. Despite all of the challenges and oppositions, Elaine remained steadfast in the belief that if we created a high-quality, rigorous school environment of excellence, parents would come, and students would thrive."

Dr. Jenkins continues with his reflection and provides greater insight and observations:

"As a visionary and strategic leader, Elaine had the uncanny ability to predict the moves of the opposition, whether they came from the DOE, a group of misinformed community members,

partisan public officials or disgruntled former staff members. Elaine was able to rally the parent and student community, engage the board members and leverage external support and advocates to push back against rumors, overstepping of policies and attempts to deny the school access to vital resources. She simply did not accept no, when it came to our quest to build a pillar of excellence in the Bronx, our shared home community. So, anyone who was along for the journey simply could not help but remain committed. We were all willingly enlisted soldiers who dedicated our time and talent to creating and sustaining International Leadership CHS. No attempts at sabotage and derailment would deter us from our ultimate goal."

When I asked John if he recalls when he first realized that International Leadership was on its way to fulfilling its mission and becoming a successful charter school, his response reflected a genuine clarity that embodied his character and depth of experience as an educator and African American male leader.

"For me, the first indication that charter school was on the trajectory to becoming one of the most successful community-grown charter high schools in the state was Elaine's unshakeable vision of excellence. Elaine began by holding an incredibly high bar for her staff. She recruited for excellent teachers, provided consistent high-quality training and professional development and remained committed to a process of performance management that either accelerated excellent practice or rooted out mediocrity and underperformance... The parents in the Bronx immediately had a place where their children were seen and treated as scholars capable of higher order thinking and advanced learning. She also built a solid and rigorous academic program

that provided a rigorous curriculum with student support to close any gaps they entered with. This formula immediately produced outstanding results as initial regents results in the first few years outpaced neighborhood high schools. International Leadership Charter HS immediately became a highly sought-after alternative for parents and students in the Bronx neighborhood it called home. I am clear that it was not accidentally. It was purposeful, intentional and strategic. Elaine has developed a model for success that is worthy of replication."

Dr. Jenkins further reflects:

"I wish that I can say that I was surprised by the relentless attacks launched against Elaine and the charter school. I wish that our nation and world history were not replete with examples of how innovative, entrepreneurial leaders who challenge power and authority are targeted for extinction. But Alas, seeking to do something that has never been achieved before often triggers fear, envy, insecurity and even rage in others. Elaine did not start International Leadership CHS to educate Black and Brown children in the traditional since. She did not want to accept any of the typical limitations around structure, resources and access that are often experienced by that population. She herself would not accept the typical treatment that women of color in leadership experience when they seek permission and approval from a male and white-culture dominant system. The building of our charter school required the creative and innovative space afforded to the creators of Microsoft, Facebook, Amazon, Netflix, Google. As she pushed for that level of agency and as we as a team lined up to support her, we upset many people who sought to create barriers and boundaries for our thinking, our access and our possibili-

ties. Thus, the typical playbook was followed: create obstacles in enrollment of students; malign the reputation of the leader; send staff in to gather intel and create sabotage; contest validity of data and results; organize resistance among disgruntled former parents and staff; change requirements and benchmarks for progress and renewal. You name it. We saw it. We conquered it! As Board Chair my role was to stand beside Elaine and the other members of the International Leadership CHS Board to form a protective hedge around the school at all costs. We knew how incredibly important the school was and would continue to be to this community and we had to be relentless in our protection of the leader, the staff and the students. I was never unclear about that calling and I never questioned my role and my purpose in that regard. As I look back, there were many scary moments. Many times I asked myself and Elaine is it worth it? Are you sure? Can we survive this? I can say then and now the answer remains a resounding YES! International Leadership CHS has continued to thrive. I and many others can drive past the beautiful edifice on Riverdale Avenue and smile, sit and gaze in silence or shed a silent tear of thanks and gratitude. For we see the manifestation of work well done; a fight hard-fought and a dream not deferred but realized. For that, I will always be proud and incredibly thankful to the friend, colleague and change maker who invited me along for the journey."

Dr. John Paul Gonzalez Gutierrez was the board chair who held the longest tenure as the board chair for the International Leadership Charter High School. Our charter school community and I also owe him a debt of gratitude for his undeniable and unwavering commitment to see the charter school grow and succeed. While writing this book, I asked him to reflect upon his journey to support the growth of our charter school that was fighting for its survival and right to exist for close to a decade. Dr. Gonzalez Gutierrez writes:

Dr. John Paul González Gutiérrez

"Our paths collided quite unexpectedly, a chance encounter with Tony López whom I knew when I was board member of Aspira, and he was the Executive Director. We engaged in a brief but impactful conversation about the power of education. In those fleeting moments, we discussed the role of schools in shaping young minds and fostering a sense of identity. Little did I know that this exchange would set in motion a sequence of events that would come to shape the very course of my journey as the Board Chair for 8 years.

It was during a follow-up meeting with Dr. Elaine Ruíz López that the pieces of the puzzle truly started to fall into place. As the discussions delved deeper, it became evident that the new school, International Leadership Charter High School, was to be a beacon of hope and change for our community. The opportunity to join the board of this emerging institution felt like an invitation to partake in a transformative endeavor, one that would touch the lives of countless individuals. As I stepped into this new role, it became apparent that the challenges we faced were far more intricate than the initial conversations had suggested. Administrative hurdles, unfairly imposed constraints, and stringent oversight from the Department of Education tested our resolve at every turn. Yet, amidst these trials, our purpose remained unswerving, a flame of determination that refused to be extinguished. The leadership provided by Dr. Elaine Ruíz López, coupled with the unwavering commitment of the board, instilled a sense of unity that fortified our mission. Together, we marched forward with an unrelenting drive to further develop an institution that would stand as a testament to the potential inherent within our community. Despite any perceived shortcomings, we were bound by a shared goal that transcended obstacles. The journey toward reauthorization was not for the faint-hearted. The process was fraught with political agendas and complex negotiations, a reminder that even the noblest of causes could become entangled in the web of bureaucracy. Yet, as a grassroots Latino-led organization, we clung to our roots, embracing our collective voice as a source of strength. Through the highs and lows, we stood firm, a united front that dared to challenge the status quo. And this was due to the inexhaustible energy of our leader and founder, Elaine."

Dr. González Gutiérrez completed a PhD in History (specializing in Puerto Rico and the Caribbean) at the Centro de Estudios Avanzados de Puerto Rico y el Caribe. He earned a BA in Music with a concentration in Music Education from the Conservatory of Music of Puerto Rico; and an MA in Teacher Education from Brooklyn College Conservatory of Music/CUNY. He completed doctoral-level coursework in Intercultural Education at NYU, and courses in Ear Training and Musicianship at the Juilliard School of Music.

CHAPTER 18

THE FIGHT FOR FISCAL EQUITY

> "Education for us, by us."
>
> **—BLACC**

According to the New York City Charter Center,[66] there are 274 charter schools in New York City today: ninety in Brooklyn, ninety-four in the Bronx, fifty-five in Manhattan, twenty-seven in Queens, and eight in Staten Island. There are 142,500 students enrolled in charter schools in NYC and 15 percent of NYC public school students attend charter schools. There are nineteen NYC charter schools (7 percent) that have collective bargaining agreements with the UFT. Our charter school is one of only eighty-six independent stand-alone schools operating in NYC.

Approximately 182,000 students attend 343 charter schools in New York State. Charter schools receive tuition payments made by school districts, funded through state and local sources; these tuition rates are established for each school district based on the average annual growth in the district's spending. Consistent with the current statutory formula, the FY 2024 Executive Budget increases New York City charter schools' per-pupil funding by 4.5 percent. This will allow

---

66   New York City Charter Center, 2023.

charter schools to continue to innovate, recruit high-quality teachers and staff, and provide strong educational options for New York's students. The FY 2024 Executive Budget also proposed to eliminate the regional cap on the number of charters that may be issued in New York City. Additionally, the executive budget proposed to permanently authorize the reissuance of any charter originally issued to a charter school that subsequently closed after July 1, 2015, due to surrender, revocation, termination, or nonrenewal. These changes will permit the issuance of additional charters in New York City and expand educational opportunities for students.

Yet, despite the record of exceptional performance and success that is well documented at a national level, in the recent release of the CREDO Study[67] and shown by the exceptional performance data collected by NYSED annually, charter schools are allocated approximately 30 percent less in per-pupil funding, as compared with what each child generates for the DOE traditional public schools. The per capita funding that was recently approved in Albany in Governor Hochul's executive budget negotiations is reported at $18,340 for charter schools. This reflects a mere 4.5 percent increase from previous allocation, as compared with the $31,434 projected 2023–2024 per-pupil spending for the traditional NYCDOE.

Remarkably, despite inequitable funding, charter schools have achieved greater results in reading and mathematics, as well as higher graduation rates with less funding, while thousands of students languish in their academic progress in districts that receive funding unconditionally, without greater accountability and without the fear of being shut down, for producing poor academic achievement outcomes.

---

67   Credo Study.

As an example of our ability to do more with less, see the chart shown for our graduation rates over the past fourteen cohorts.

REPRESENTATION MATTERS

The legislative advocacy groups that support charter schools in New York State have been tireless in advocating for equity in funding and support for the lifting of the cap on charter schools. These include the New York Charter School Association (NYCSA), the National Alliance for Public Charter Schools (NAPCS), and the Black Latinx Asian Charter Collaborative (BLACC).

According to Ron Rice, senior director of Government Relations for the NAPCS,[68] "*The debate on public education has never been louder and the time is now for Congress to truly listen to the nation's public charter school leaders of color. These leaders, who are teachers, principals, advocates, and community members, know firsthand how the charter school model successfully provides a high-quality education to the children and families in their communities, and especially to students of color. In addition, charter schools historically serve proportionately more students of color and more students from low-income communities than district schools.*"

NAPCS also reports that in the most recently available data (2020–2021 school year), 60 percent of charter school students participate in the federal free and reduced-price lunch program, compared to 53 percent of district school students. According to data from the National Center for Education Statistics, 31.5 percent of charter schoolteachers and 33.4 percent of charter school leaders are people of color compared to 19.3 and 21.8 percent, respectively, in district public schools.

---

68   National Alliance for Public Charter Schools. February 28, 2023.

BLACK LATINX ASIAN CHARTER COLLABORATIVE (BLACC)

"Education for us, by us."

Founded in 2018 by charter school educators of color in New York City, the BLACC exists to ensure that all families of color in the state of New York can access excellent, high-quality public charter schools. Among BLACC's founders are the most brilliant and dedicated charter school leaders of color who had the boldness of an idea to harness the principles of "Education for us and by us." They include Reverend Al Cockfield, Dr. Charlene Reid, Dr. Steve Perry, Dr. Vasthi Acosta, Rafiq Kalan Id-din, Dominique Lee, and Miriam Raccah.

BLACC is now a nonprofit organization dedicated to elevating charter schools founded and led by people of color in New York City. It represents educators and stakeholders in the community who, through our shared experiences, acknowledge a hopeful opportunity in the sector: community-based schools founded by leaders of color are powerful vehicles for change and progress. While many local and national organizations seek to advance the interests of public charter schools, BLACC is the only organization specifically supporting the success and growth of new and existing public charter schools led by educators of color in the state of New York.

The organization works together with local charter schools to ensure that the needs of our communities are at the forefront of education reform. Today, BLACC is a membership-driven organization that represents over twenty charter schools and over thirteen thousand students.

According to Miriam Raccah, CEO for BLACC, the motto "education for us, by us" is embedded in the belief that every aspect of their work, from whom they serve to what they advocate for, is rooted in the profound conviction that communities of color have the right to engage in self-determination, especially when it comes to the education of our children. Ms. Raccah writes:

> *"For decades, communities of color have protested the ongoing failure of the traditional system when it comes to educating children of color. And while the system as a whole continues to consistently fail our children, we, as an organization founded by public charter school educators, understand what is possible in public schooling when increased autonomy and flexibility are granted in exchange for accountability for academic outcomes. And while we and all educators of color have always known that culturally affirming schools positively shape the educational lives of students of color, as a country we now have ample and irrefutable empirical evidence of the long-term impact that leaders and teachers of color have on the academic and life trajectory of children of color."*

Ms. Raccah also emphasizes the thwarted growth potential of the charter school sector that is led by educators of color, given that there is a cap on the number of charter schools that can be established in NYC due to the staunch political opposition from the UFT and the traditional Democrats in the Assembly, as well as the Senate, who depend on union support and campaign dollars. On behalf of all charter schools that are led by leaders of color, Ms. Raccah makes an appeal to the philanthropic community to increase the funding of charter schools led by leaders of color. In a report[69] that outlines BLACC's strategic vision to meet this long-term goal in public education, she writes:

---

69   Black Latinx Asian Charter Collaborative, 2023.

"Creating a clear path for equitable access to funding will not only help current leaders of color to improve their programs (and potentially incentivize them to stay in their roles), but by outlining a clear ecosystem for funding, it will also attract more leaders and teachers of color into the New York public charter school space, which will ultimately increase quality and continue to ensure the long-term viability of the charter sector. As such, while we believe in the potential of the public charter school model, we know that in order to fully catalyze its power, we need to move the needle on increasing the number of public charter schools led and staffed by people of color. We also know that without shifting the movement to be predominantly led by leaders of color, the politics surrounding charter schools, particularly in progressive-leaning states like New York, will not only result in the dampening and/or stalling of near- and long-term seat growth, it also poses an existential threat to the viability and relevance of public charter schools over time."

Latino Charter Leaders Roundtable (LCLR) at the BLACC Gala
Anthony López, Suzanna De Leon, Cindy Lopez, Dr. Elaine Ruíz López, Melissa
Melkonian, Bishop Raymond Rivera

LATINO CHARTER LEADERS ROUNDTABLE

Amber Charter School was founded in New York City in the year 2000 by Evelyn Marzan and Jon Moscow. It is the first Latino-led charter school in the state. In its almost twenty-five years of existence, it has grown from a small, one-campus kindergarten school in East Harlem to a network of K-8 schools (East Harlem, Kingsbridge, and Inwood). Dr. Vasthi R. Acosta led the school from 2007 to 2022 and grew it to become a network of schools. During Dr. Acosta's tenure as executive director of Amber Charter Schools, her two greatest accomplishments were the growth of the school from one campus to three campuses and developing the leaders that would succeed after her tenure. This career ladder helped to foster an organizational culture of enthusiasm, constant learning, and high retention of staff. Therefore, it was the greatest moment of pride for Dr. Acosta when her successors were home-grown leaders that had worked at Amber for over fifteen years.

One of the greatest challenges Dr. Acosta faced, as the leader of Amber Charter Schools, came early in her tenure. Within a year of her taking on the leadership, the authorized SUNY CSI announced to the Board of Trustees that they would shut down Amber unless the state test scores were increased within the year. Amber had one year to prove to the authorizer that they could raise student test scores and deserved to exist. After implementing over nine different initiatives to turn the school around, the student test scores increased by 30 points in both math and English language arts. The school was saved from being shut down. Dr. Acosta writes:

> *"Leadership is lonely. Dr. Acosta found herself desiring the counsel of other leaders and feeling the pressure of leading all alone. To meet her need for the companionship of other leaders and under*

the advice of Rossana Rosado, who at the time was the publisher
of El Diario/La Prensa (the largest tristate Spanish language
newspaper). I sent out an invitation to as many Latino charter
leaders as she could find to join her for a conversation in the hope
of establishing a group of leaders who could support one another
in their quest to successfully educate black and brown children".

The Latino Charter Leaders Roundtable (LCLR) was convened and founded in 2012. LCLR met every month through the pandemic of 2020–2021. In addition to Amber, the LCLR leaders represented the International Leadership Charter High School, FLACS, Yonkers Charter School for Educational Excellence, Heketi, WHIN, and American Dream. The leaders of these school shared challenges, knowledge, expertise, counsel, and support through hardships, friendship, and camaraderie through the monthly meetings. According to Dr. Acosta, LCLR inspired the creation of BLACC. As one of the founding members, Dr. Acosta viewed BLACC to expand the reach and influence of more charter leaders of color.

In June of 2022 when Vashti retired as CEO of Amber Charter School, she asked me to consider leading LCLR. Although apprehensive, I accepted this new challenge by faith and continue the legacy of support for our colleagues.[70]

---

70   Latino Charter Leaders Roundtable, https://www.latinocharterleadersroundtable. com/.

CHAPTER 19

THE ALUMNI AND LEGACY

"Changing Lives, Transforming Communities
One Scholar at a Time."
—DR. ELAINE RUÍZ LÓPEZ

would like to share with you a sampling of the "Dear Dr. Ruíz López" letters I have received over the years. The words of the alumni echo the essence of our shared experiences, reflections of the transformative journeys woven within the fabric of the International Leadership Charter High School. Their narratives are the true markers of the impact and success of our collective endeavors, shining lights on the paths we've traversed together. It's a heartfelt honor to have been a part of their journeys, to have witnessed the unfolding of their potentials, and to have shared in their aspirations, challenges, and triumphs. Each testimonial is a reminder of the boundless possibilities that lie within every student and the transformative power of education when imbued with passion, dedication, and love. They serve as enduring inspirations, fueling the continual quest for educational excellence and the unwavering commitment to nurturing the leaders of tomorrow. What follows is a selection of the Dear Dr. López Letters.

BRANDON AQUINO

Class of 2020 Valedictorian

Throughout four years as a student at International Leadership Charter High School I have developed and gained many new useful skills that can benefit me in my future and in college your dedication and motivation help push me to strike for the best and to perform the best in school international leadership helped develop my social skills leadership availability and to perform the best in any task the many rigorous classes challenge me to do my best and achieve the highest grades possible these classes help prepare me for the difficult classes I will have to take in college and I know that I will not struggle as much because the course is prepared me mentally and academically to successfully complete assignments with high passing grades. I am grateful for all the teachers that you chose that motivated me challenged me and never let me give up on achieving my short- and long-term goals thank you for everything have done for me to make sure I succeed in college and be successful for the rest of my life.

JAILYN ALEXIS RUÍZ

Class of 2020—Student Advisory Council Leader

I would like to take this opportunity to express my gratitude to you and thank you so much for the kind help and support you provided to me as well as a good learning environment. Your words of encouragement and advice during the school year helped push me to where I am today. Not only was I a part of the Model United Nations but I was also part of the Scales of Justice Academy, led by Judge LaTia Martin during a three-week summer program. Through this program at Fordham University law school I was educated on many broad matter matters related to law professions. I was also given the opportunity to develop skills that will be essential to success in any future career I choose such as new ways of thinking, new locations and public speaking. I want to thank you for promoting an environment where I feel like I'm I am able to not only share my ideas and make a contribution but also know, it is actually considered and appreciated I was able to be part of a student council and I know it is something that I've contributed to the school that will be passed down to other grades and graduating classes.

ANDREW RIVAS

Class of 2020

"I would like to say what an honor it was to attend International Leadership Charter High School. This school has made me achieve my full potential in school. Learning in this school has made me focus on my goals and made me do more in life. I would like to explain to you why I am so thankful for this opportunity. The International Leadership Charter HS, is a great school in my opinion. The academics are great, and it is a safe environment, I have learned so much these past four years, and our teachers have shown us care and have helped us succeed. I think this school is great as it has made me more responsible and more independent. I value this school so much due to it giving me a more focused mindset on achieving any type of goal I have. Finally, I have learned that if you want something, strive for it and work hard. I am grateful that this school has made me work hard toward graduation. I would like to pursue a Computer Science degree at the University of Miami. If I had not attended this school, I would not be where I am now and would not be accepted into this school or would have the ability to be the best version of myself. Thank you Dr. López, may God bless you."

BRYANNA MOLINA

Class of 2021

"I would like to thank you for your dedication to my education. I am also thankful for the programs that have been implemented here, such as the band program and Taekwondo. Being part of the band program for a part of my freshman year was a good creative outlet to have, and Taekwondo was a good change to our everyday routine and a chance to be active. Returning to in-person learning was nerve-racking at first, but I appreciate the whole staff's effort to make everyone feel safe in the building. Applying to college this year was a unique experience. The pandemic prevented everyone from visiting colleges in person and make connections with admissions counselors in a traditional way. I am grateful that we were able to visit schools virtually during our class time and that we got to ask admissions counselors any questions that we had. The college application process was made much easier for us in a time of great uncertainty and stress, which I am very thankful for. Overall, I have made many great memories at this school, and I am grateful for the time I have spent here."

ASHLEY FERNANDEZ

Class of 2022 Valedictorian

"You have provided so many opportunities for me so I can pass all my classes. Even though, during 2020 it was difficult because Covid-19 but I was able to go through it and attend school. Also, I was scared at first of coming back to school for junior year, but you made sure that we would be safe and healthy. Spending 4 years in school was the best time of my life. From freshman year to junior year, I had been receiving honor rolls and my grades were improving so much because I had always put my

education first before anything else. I am transitioning to the next 4 years to a college education. I had never thought until 11th grade that there was a chance for me to be able to receive college credits to transfer to a college I will be attending.

Now it is my little brother's chance to spend the rest of his 4 years in the school to be able to receive the same requirements that I had before graduating. education."

AMELIA ALMONTE

Class of 2022 Salutatorian

"I would like to personally thank you, Dr. López, for taking full charge of my education and leading me through this journey. Firstly, I would like to thank you for offering me the chance to complete a computer science program at Stanford University. This program helped me expand my knowledge and learn from teachers at an Ivy League school. I was able to learn how to build and design my own website. In addition to learning how to protect my personal information from unauthorized pages. This would not have been possible without your efforts and contributions. This experience has led me to being accepted at Barnard College at Columbia University. I would also like to thank you for correctly managing the pandemic. It was a stressful time for most of us, however, you made sure we were protected against the virus. While other schools were fully online, we were able to share with our teachers and classmates. This journey would have been more complex without your dedication. Thank you for always making sure we were stepping in the right direction."

KIARALYS RIVERA

Class of 2022

"I want to take this opportunity to personally thank you for being there for me at a time I needed emotional support. We both lost a loved one and having someone that could understand my feelings and emotions was incredibly special to me. It did happen a while ago, but that gesture profoundly impacted me in an effective way because I felt like I had the support and a piece of what it would be like to still have her here with us. Not only with me, but I saw how you encouraged and motivated every one of us to do better in the Taekwondo promotion test whenever Plan A and Plan B failed. Coming to ILCHS was originally not in my plan book, but these past four years have proven that everything does have a purpose, and everything does happen for a reason."

BRAYHAN MORROBEL

Class of 2022

"Primarily, I would like to commend you for all your work at the International Leadership Charter High School. I admire the organization and the tidiness that has been kept in the school throughout all the four years that I have been a student here. Thanks to your leadership, we have all developed skills that will serve as a foundation for our futures. You have shown us many things. You have shown us that Latina women do have a chance to be successful in this world. You have shown us to be organized. You have shown us to be responsible. But most importantly of all, you have shown us how to change the world. You have completed your goal: ... that elevates students' intellectual capacity" and your goal of "formando minorias."

You have provided us with many opportunities, despite how COVID-19 and the pandemic have complicated things. You brought us the amazing opportunity to be part of the Stanford University computer science program, which was difficult, but it was worth it as I learned how to make a website. I would like you to know that I am extremely grateful for the recommendation letter that you wrote for me. The future is bright, I will be able to look back and say, "I was a student at International Leadership Charter High School," and I will be proud.

IAN BERMUDEZ
Valedictorian, Class of 2023

"Safety is something I never have to worry about when I step into school, and I would like to personally thank you for the effort you have put into furthering my education. Through your exemplary leadership, you have given me the opportunity to seek higher education at several world-renowned institutions across the country. Even through the tragedy of Covid-19 tainting my first year, I was able to persevere and educate myself due to policies put in place by you. My experience in this school has been pivotal in my life. It has given me exposure to the real world and has prepared me for what life has to offer me. I am extremely grateful because you have given me the opportunity to meet many lifelong friends and made me a part of a marvelous community. Determination is a character trait that has been implemented into me through the leadership you instilled into every scholar that has stepped foot into this fine establishment. I am proud to say I attended International Leadership Charter High School!"

TRIANA BAUTISTA

Salutatorian, Class of 2023

"I am profoundly grateful for the opportunities you have given me throughout my years at the International Leadership Charter School. We can all agree that the past years were anything but easy. As soon as COVID hit, high school was less than ordinary. The school always assured me that even though the pandemic was taking its course my academics would not be affected. Something I always appreciated was the diversity the school has to offer. Coming into this High School was the first time I felt represented. I had teachers and consolers that understood me and looked like me. I did not feel like a minority in a classroom. I often acknowledge the support you have given students finding the best education they can have. You never frowned on the likelihood of a student's ability to excel and be a leader in the outside world. The opportunities you have given students push them to believe that they can accomplish endless possibilities and think the impossible. As I leave this school and go into the real world, I hope that the students that will sit in the same seats as I, will acknowledge the everlasting effect you have had through your support."

AISSATOU SYLLA

Class of 2023

"I would like to start with a thank you. Thank you for all the direct and indirect things that you have done for me and my classmates When I came to this school, it was my first time in the United States altogether. I was lost and nervous to enter this building or even speak to anyone. I thought that I was not going to be able to understand any of the lessons taught in class or even make any friends. Fortunately, ILCHS had a lot to offer me. All the teachers worked together to make sure that I understood everything

THE ALUMNI AND LEGACY

been explained. Moreover, I would like to thank you for everything you have been doing to improve our high school experience through all the events and opportunities that we were given this year. I want to make sure you know that all your hard work is not going to be wasted and it is appreciated. From me and all the seniors of this year, we are profoundly grateful and thankful for everything that you have done and continues to do for us."

DANDRE BENJAMIN DELEON

Class of 2023

"I am extremely grateful for this school and the chances it has given me now that I am a senior. Although I was terrified and anxious to enter a new school with individuals I had not met before, as you have demonstrated to us that a number or graph does not define who we are, you have given us several opportunities and resources to achieve in life and to develop as great individuals. The COVID-19 virus was one of many obstacles my class of 2023 faced in the educational system, but you gave us a sense of strength that allowed us to press through. Thank you, Dr. López, for providing us with so many possibilities to advance our education and choose our career paths. You have built a fantastic school and selected a fantastic faculty. I appreciate how you constantly challenge us to reach our greatest potential. Without this school, I would not be the person I am today. It is safe to say that the young people at this institution did not regret the experiences that our persuasive CEO gave them. You are the institution's hero and its soul—a fantastic example of what we are all supposed to be. Given the numerous chances we were given and will always value, it has been an honor to be a student at International Leadership Charter High School."

TUKU GAYE
Class of 2023

"I appreciate the decisions you made with the best interests of our students in mind. International Leadership Charter High School's success is built on your labor of love. Thank you so much for your kind help, support you provided us, and a good learning environment. Your words of encouragement and advice during assemblies helped most of us students to be where we are today. Your influence on our lives will always be remembered. Thank you, Dr. López, for always prioritizing us and working to raise the standard of our instruction. You are a source of motivation, inspiration, and support. I received 7 college credits through the College Now program with Lehman College. The Bioengineering internship with Stanford University gave me the opportunity to experience a college course class at an early start which will prepare me for college."

EDILIS GONZALEZ
Alumni Parent, Class of 2010

Edilis Gonzalez was my first hire and a proud parent of an alumni who graduated with our first cohort in 2010. Eighteen years later, she is still working with me side by side as Director of Parent Engagement and has been an essential stakeholder in achieving our charter school mission and goals. Edilis writes in her reflection:

My name is Edilis Gonzalez, I was born in the Dominican Republic on November 16, 1971. I am number nine in a family of ten, married and have two daughters, Stephany Richely Gonzalez, 30 years old, and Edith Lisbeth Gonzalez, 28 years old.

In 2006 Stephany was ready to enter high school but she was assigned to one of the worst HS in the Bronx, due to the zip code where I lived at that time. As a mother, I was desperate and very worried about my daughter's safety and the type of education she was going to receive since that school was full of gangs, violence and overcrowded with more than 4 thousand students in total. My daughter would be just another number and I was sure that she would not be successful. Due to my economic situation, I could not pay for a private school and I was not able to ensure that my daughter received any scholarship for her secondary education. I was more desperate every day as I saw that the days were getting closer and I couldn't find a solution. My prayers were constant asking God for a solution. One day God gave the answer and I found an invitation in my mailbox from a new charter school that was opening soon and was going to meet at the neighborhood library to talk to the parents. My eyes filled with tears and I just said God, that's my daughter's school, "thank you." I was one of the first people to arrive at the library and fill out an application for my daughter. That day I saw Dr. López and some people who would work at this school, which at that time did not have an address, much less an assigned school building.

Regardless of how long I had to wait, I knew that this was my daughter's school. A few days later I received the news that they had rented a space and that we were invited to see it. That day was a Wednesday (I will never forget it). I was the first person to arrive at that place. I introduced myself to the Doctor. López and while she showed me around, I told her my story and at the same time expressed my gratitude for opening this school that would save my daughter's life and educational future. While we were walking and talking, she turned around and looked me in the eyes and she told me "I would like to have someone like you in this place to work with me" and she immediately asked me what level of education I had. My heart raced and, surprised, I responded, I'm at Bronx Community College, I'm very close to graduating, I speak English. I was working as a Home Health Aide caring for the elderly. She asked me to send my resume and the next day she sent it to her. She immediately responded inviting me to go see her. When I arrived, she interviewed me and offered me the job as a School Aide which I was delighted to accept. My daughter Stephany and I started on the same day, she as a student at the first HS in the Bronx and I as an employee at International Leadership Charter High School. That day Dr. López changed my daughter's life, mine and that of my entire family forever. My daughter Stephany graduated from school with honors and today she is a successful woman with a master's degree, married, mother of three children and works in a school. Today I look back and it's been 18 years. Today I am Director of Parent and School Community Engagement, and I can only say thank you very much for so many opportunities to grow as a person and professionally. Her constant support, guidance, and advice made me who I am today. Dr. López is more than my teacher, she is part of my family. I keep in my heart immense gratitude, feelings of admiration and respect for the founder and school leader. She changed my life, that of my daughter and my family forever!

These testimonies documented in the previous pages from the alumni are just a representation of the hundreds of letters and expressions of gratitude received over nearly two decades. It is my belief that the greatest form of gratitude is that the alumni will become the leaders that the borough of the Bronx need and that they will become the change and the champions for equity and social justice in education, housing, healthcare, peace in our neighborhoods, and above all role models for their children and the youth of this city. Many of the alumni from cohorts 2010–2019 have already graduated from college and have embarked upon their careers. It is my desire that all of the alumni will be inspired to pay it forward and write their own stories. They will carry out my legacy and vision for the Bronx.

A s I wrote this epilogue, my first thought was that this story does not have a finite ending. This journey continues through the life and aspirations of the parents and alumni who are the leaders of the next decade and beyond. The story of the *International Leadership Charter High School* as the first charter high school in the Bronx will continue to evolve through future generations and will become part of the fabric of the myriad of stories of leaders and educators born and raised in the Bronx in similar neighborhoods, who chose to remain and speak up for what is right and to become the change. The fight for equity in the Bronx and to change lives and transform communities one scholar at a time was born out of a deep desire to improve the lives and social economic circumstances that Puerto Ricans, Dominicans, African Americans, and all children of immigrants of Afro Caribbean heritage deserve.

Abuela Zenobia

I am a Puerto Rican woman of color, and I embrace my heritage and honor my African roots. My maternal grandmother and matriarch *Zenobia Ortiz* born in 1895 was of West African descent. She was

Grand Aunt Carmen Rodriguez Bosch (this is Rosario's sister)

married to *Rosario Urutia Bosch* who was of Catalan Spaniard heritage. In my search over the last thirty years, I learned that her father, my great-grandfather, at the age of nine, was taken from Nigeria along with my great-great-grandmother *Fermina* and three siblings. They were stolen from their homeland in West Africa and brought to Puerto Rico against their will as slaves, where they were sold to toil on a sugar and coffee plantation in Yauco, owned by Francisco Lluveras and his family. The diaspora and African roots of our people was not a popular topic for discussion among many Puerto Rican families. There was always a sense of shame that I later identified as internalized oppression. The focus of our history and ancestry was always on the white Spaniard European side. This relationship was romanticized along with the Taino indigenous side of our heritage. Our African ancestry was minimized as unimportant and rarely, if ever, honored. It was only after I started asking my mother where we were from and about our ancestors that she began to open up and shared that my great-grandfather was African, who spoke in a dialect that she could not always understand. This was never discussed, and it took years of oral history and conducting research till I learned the truth about the great-grandfather Baba (Papa) Uyo that my mother would quietly share stories about. The practice by the slave masters was to strip Africans of their birth names and give them the surnames of the plantation owners, which would be physically branded onto their skin with hot iron tools. Throughout his adult life, Baba Uyo was known as Guillermo Lluveras. At death, his birth certificate did not reflect his owner's last name but that of the woman that he married, my great-grandmother, *Valentina del Coral Ortiz*. I never met my maternal grandparents; however, I was able to obtain the one and only photograph that existed of my maternal grandmother on a trip to visit my cousin in Guayanilla, Puerto Rico. Her photograph reflects her strength, a life of struggle, hardship, and indignation. She raised three daughters and a son and became the caretaker of all of her grandchildren at some point. The history of slavery in Puerto Rico and the Caribbean has left generational scars and a resilience, strength, and determination in Afro Boricuas. Despite the hundreds of years of violence, trauma, anger, and pain that began with the Spanish conquistadores our people have become great leaders, cultural artists, philosophers, educators, doctors, authors, and historians.

As a child born and raised in the South Bronx in a poor working-class neighborhood, although aware of the dangers I was at the same time conditioned and desensitized to my surroundings through my late teens. I am a survivor of childhood and generational trauma, a racially hostile environment in the healthcare and education system, domestic violence, and a neighborhood that was going up in flames for a decade. I was a witness to the crushing of the human spirit in the Bronx due to the cruelty of mental illness, crime, sexual molestation, substance abuse, and the AIDS/HIV crisis. As an adolescent and throughout my life, I have been personally impacted or affected by all of these conditions directly or indirectly. These social diseases did not spare any family including that of my own. The sad reality is that these diseases continue to destroy dreams, threaten the well-being of children, and tear families apart. However, I have great optimism that through access to a quality education, pathways to college, and the development of our youth as leaders, the future generations will work to transform hopelessness into endless possibilities. A higher education provided me with the lifeline to climb out from under my personal circumstances when I found myself drowning as an eighteen-year-old teenage mom of a two-year-old, it was my return to the pursuit of education that saved me and equipped me, to support thousands of children and families who needed an alternative to what the NYC public school system was offering. For migrant and immigrant families, the way out of their circumstances and their future is often in the hands of their children. One hundred percent of the families that I have met over the past eighteen years had a dream for their child. My goal in writing this inspirational memoir and telling the story of my journey has many dimensions. I am a woman of faith and believe that it was indeed divine intervention that suddenly appeared with a ladder of opportunity to help me to climb out of the social chaos of the streets and economic despair. Enrolling in college at the age of eighteen years despite the insurmountable challenges was the lifeline that would put me on a path toward becoming a teacher in my early twenties, fueling the desire to return to the South Bronx, while pursuing graduate degrees and a doctorate from TC at Columbia University. This is just a small part of the story. I have shared the extraordinary challenges that I was confronted with when opening and leading a charter school, in order to encourage the reader to persevere, and to pursue your God-given passion and purpose for this one amazing life that we have. Whether you are an educator, administrator, a businessperson, community activist, in law enforce-ment, an attorney, doctor, parent, or college student, the pursuit of the most difficult road instead of what is convenient will teach you more about yourself and what your purpose is on this planet. I now stand on the other side of what appeared to be impossible, to find thousands of children and a community who were waiting for a champion that had the courage to fight for what is possible and to make their dreams a reality. As a child and a teenage mom at sixteen years of age, who was pushed out of high school, I never imagined that I would graduate from college, become a teacher, complete my doctorate from an Ivy League university, and decades later lead one of the most successful charter schools in the Bronx.

Refusing rejection was a skill and a muscle that I learned to develop. Failure and giving up the fight for equity in education for our youth was not an option. At every turn since our beginning in 2005, there have been challenges and obstacles to overcome in the establishment of our charter school. There were bureaucrats both in the NYC public system and at NYSED who were the designated gate-keepers, who fought against our innovative work with students and were ready to block any real change that would challenge the status quo, and were committed to say "*No, you can't.*" My brain could not process this, and my heart would respond "*Why not?*"

The sting of rejection was a constant and unwelcome intruder. In the process, I learned numerous lessons that only fueled my desire to keep on going and not give up. My drive was born out of a vision that was of a far greater power than any of the doors that would close. I learned how to reject rejection and refused to allow the dream killers to paralyze the plans for a school that was ordained by GOD and meant to happen. The countless rejections became the motivation to succeed and go farther. I have heard many ministers say a setback is only a setup for greater things to come. I agree with all my heart. For every door that was slammed shut, a window opened that gave me a second wind to continue the fight and to endure till I achieved my goals.

We had to be intentional about going from good to great and will continue to strive for this ideal. Although extremely proud of our accomplishments, I am the toughest critic and we are not there yet. By the first renewal in 2011 our charter school had demonstrated clear and irrefutable evidence: we outperformed all the neighboring district schools, as well as the city and the state with our high graduation rates and excellent performance on the NYS Regents exam. We received our second renewal in 2015 from the DOE and in 2016 moved into a beautifully designed permanent private space that was built with municipal bond financing that currently stands on a prominent corner on Riverdale Avenue and West 231st Street, in the northern sector of District 10. Since 2016 we have been recognized consistently by US NEWS & WORLD REPORT.

My faith and constant prayers that "mountains be moved" sustained me through the past eighteen years. After an exhausting battle with the DOE the first five years, we were granted a second charter term that was filled with microaggressions and simple indifference to our vision and goals. Even though our charter school continued to be one of the highest performing community-grown charter schools in the Bronx and the city, we received no accolades and little support or guidance from our DOE authorizer when faced with obstacles. In 2016, the Board of Trustees and I were ready for the change, so we took another leap of faith and started to explore the opportunity to transfer authorizers from DOE to SUNY CSI, notwithstanding that SUNY had a reputation for being the tougher authorizer with higher levels of accountability, with renewals that were either zero or five years. A few of my colleagues, namely Dr. Vasthi Acosta and Marilyn Calo, led charter schools authorized by SUNY and reassured me that this greater accountability also came with guidance, support, as well as greater flexibility and objectivity. Although apprehensive, we were not afraid of accountability and knew that we had to work smarter and meet their expectations. This was a chance that we were willing to take. In 2017 we successfully transferred authorizer status from DOE to SUNY. It was among the best decisions that the board made, and since then, doors of opportunities opened for us to expand student seats and grow.

In our darkest days, we could see light at the end of the tunnel. On March 11, 2020, only a few days before schools were shut down by the COVID-19 pandemic, our charter school was renewed for a third charter term and by SUNY for the first time. Like many, the pandemic loomed over us as thousands of people were becoming ill and dying from COVID in the Bronx and throughout NYC. All schools were shut down as the city went dark, while bodies were being lined up to be loaded alongside waiting refrigerated trucks. In those chilling moments, the last thing on my mind and list of priorities was to build another charter school. In April of 2020, I received an invitation from the Walton Family Foundation (WFF) about expanding our school, with an invitation to apply for the *Accelerating Emerging Charter Network* grant. The timing of the invitation seemed incongruent to the new reality of living in a pandemic. Like many, I was afraid and shellshocked by the lives lost and the isolation from the world that we once knew. My priority was keeping myself and husband healthy and COVID free, staying in touch with our family and the school's leadership team, and providing students and families with technology, meals, and updated information from the CDC and the New York State Department of Health (NYSDOH). We maintained our close connection and we reopened in September of 2020. We knew how important it was to provide support to our entire community in every way possible. I also needed to come up with a plan for the class of 2020 graduation. We had no choice but to cancel their prom. With the support of the Bronx Borough President's Office and my dear friend and fellow Bronxite, Marlene Cintron, president of BOEDC, and Olga Luz Tirado, formerly Bronx Tourism Council, I was teamed up with an architect who designed the specs and permissions from the Department of Buildings for a tent on the lawn of the College of Mount Saint Vincent's in Riverdale where all ten of the previous cohort commencement exercises were held. The regulations called for no greater than 150 people in attendance, proof of a COVID test, and mandatory masks. Remarkably, we were able to graduate our resilient class of 2020 who wore matching masks on a very hot day in June. It was yet another miracle, I thought, as I looked up the steps to a very powerful sight to where our scholars were all lined up waiting for me to start the commencement exercises. There was not a dry eye in the room. As the CEO and superintendent of this charter school district, the uncertainty of the times weighed heavily on me, and the anxiety levels were high. I decided that I needed another project to look forward to, so I applied to the WFF for the grant, and we were selected. We were awarded close to $1 million to expand to include a middle school and to replicate our high school. We then obtained approval from the SUNY Board of Trustees for expansion in June of 2021.

The resolution presented to the SUNY CSI Board of Trustees follows below:

> "International Leadership has high rates of absolute and comparative graduation achievement. Over the last five school years, the school graduates students at rates that exceeded the local district and SUNY's absolute target of 75% each year. Notably in 2017/18, 95% of the school's 2014 Graduation Cohort graduated after four years exceeding the district performance by 19 points. Similarly in 2019/20, 94.2% of

the 2016 Graduation Cohort graduated on time, beating the district by 14.2%. The school demonstrated a strong record of college preparation over the same period. In 2017/18 and 2018/19, the school matriculated 99% of its graduates each year into a two- or four-year college program after graduation surpassing SUNY's target of 75%. In spring 2020, 21 International Leadership graduates enrolled at SUNY schools. In 2019/20, 97% of the school's graduates matriculated after graduation. The school also posted high achievement in English language arts ("ELA") and mathematics over the period. Notably, 71% of the school's 2015 Total Cohort achieved at least Level 4 on the Regents ELA exam surpassing the district results by 18 points."

INTERNATIONAL LEADERSHIP CHARTER HIGH SCHOOL

Four-Year Graduation Rates (2010-2023)

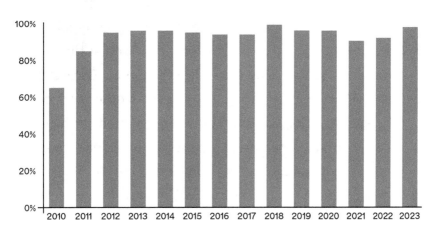

Data Source: APPR SUNY CSI; NYSED; International Leadership CHS Data

Since receiving the WFF grant we have received matching funds from Bloomberg philanthropies to support our expansion. On September 11, 2023, we celebrated the inauguration of our middle school in a 104-year-old Catholic school building that we renovated while we waited for the completion of our permanent facility in the Kingsbridge neighborhood. In attendance were members of the school community who have supported us over the past eighteen years to include parent leaders, our board, future scholars, middle school faculty, and leadership.

Despite the resounding support from *Parents United for the International Leadership Charter Schools*, Assemblyman Jeffrey Dinowitz has taken sides with the anti-charter school group of individuals who have launched a *"Stop the Charter School Build Campaign."* He has turned his back on his own constituents - hundreds of students and families of color who vote!

Our construction site has been vandalized simultaneous to strategy meetings to intentionally derail our timeline for construction led by the NY Teachers Coop at Tibbets Towers on West 232nd Street. This Not in My Backyard (NIMBY) group is opposing the right to an education for students of color, while a few of these detractors have taken it upon themselves to cut security wires, glue locks and prevent our crews from completing their work. This has slowed down our timeline by 18 months.

Unfortunately, after Ruben Diaz, Jr. Former Bronx Borough President moved on, we no longer have the courageous leadership that we once enjoyed and any politician bold enough to confront the racism and the pattern of red lining and discrimination being perpetuated in this sector of the Bronx, by Assemblyman Dinowitz. The former Assemblyman Marcos Crespo was our champion in the Assembly for charter schools and moved on leaving a vacuum in leadership and advocacy for charter schools. We have optimism that our future legislators may be among our alumni and parents, who will run for office on a pro charter school platform.

Our families are low-income and working-class from LatinX, African American, African and Caribbean communities looking for a quality education for their children. We cannot allow "nimbyism" to deny an education to middle school students who live in the Kingsbridge community and deserve this opportunity to receive a quality education.[71]

---

71   Susan Edelman, "Once Again, the UFT Sides against Parents and Kids," New York Post, May 17, 2023, https://nypost.com/2023/05/17/once-again-the-uft-sides-against-parents-and-kids/, accessed January 20, 2024.;
Stacy Driks, "International Leadership: We've Had Enough," The Riverdale Press, May 19, 2023, https://www.riverdalepress.com/stories/international-leadership-weve-had-enough,110399, accessed January 20, 2024.;
Susan Edelman, "Bronx Pols Fight Construction of Charter School in Kingsbridge," New York Post, May 21, 2023, https://nypost.com/2023/05/21/bronx-pols-fight-construction-of-charter-school-in-kingsbridge/, accessed January 20, 2024.;
Stacy Driks, "Proposed Charter Middle School Raises Tension," The Riverdale Press, January 20, 2023, https://www.riverdalepress.com/stories/proposed-charter-middle-school-raises-tension,107169, accessed January 20, 2024.;
Kate Taylor, "Racial Bias at a Bronx School," The New York Times, October 5, 2016, https://www.nytimes.com/2016/10/06/nyregion/bronx-public-school-racial-bias.html, accessed January 20, 2024.

CHANGE IS COMING: THE ALUMNI— OUR FUTURE LEADERS

Today we have three alumni from the class of 2017 and one from the class of 2020 who are now working as members of the team at the charter school. Paola Carrion (2017) graduated from Saint John's University and is working as a guidance counselor. Luis Beltre graduated from Mercy University (2017) and is working in school operations. Brandon Aquino, our 2020 class valedictorian, is working as a teacher associate while he works to complete his degree at CCNY

Alumni Joel and Luis Beltre with Dr. Elaine Ruíz López

where he plans to pursue a master's degree in psychology. This was part of the vision for our charter school that alumni would have a desire to return and give back to the community and support and sustain the charter school's great success.

In the heart of the Bronx, we've established this charter school not just as a testament to our struggle but as a beacon of hope, change, and progress. Thank you to all who worked with me to create this vision. Remember, no dream is too lofty, no effort in vain. With determination and courage, the impossible becomes possible. Let this charter inspire all to believe in the power of fighting for equity to change lives and transform communities one scholar at a time.

I end this epilogue by giving honor to my mother Lucila, who came to the United States from Puerto Rico with an ninth grade education. She sacrificed it all for her children and inspired me to keep on going, and never stop dreaming.

Class of 2010

Class of 2011

Class of 2012

Class of 2013

Class of 2014

Class of 2015

Class of 2016

Class of 2017

Class of 2018

Class of 2019

Class of 2020

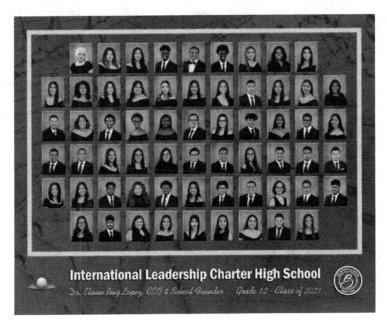

Class of 2021

Class of 2022

Class of 2023

Class of 2024

Outdoor Graduation Class of 2020 at College of Mount Saint Vincent

TRIBUTE TO LUCILA, MI MADRE

I give honor to my mother Lucila, who came to the United States from Puerto Rico having barely completed a 9th grade education. She sacrificed it all for a better future and her children. She inspired me to keep on going, and never stop dreaming.

Lucila Ruíz Rodriguez, Graduation from MobiCentrics Mature Workers Program, 1985

DR. ELAINE RUÍZ LÓPEZ

Dr. Elaine Ruíz López is the founder and the chief executive officer of the International Leadership Charter High School. Dr. Ruíz López was born and raised in the South Bronx and is first generation Puerto Rican and first in her family to graduate from college. She has worked in the field of education since 1980. During her career, she has held various leadership positions in public schools and universities. She earned her Doctorate in Special Education/Administration and second Masters of Education from the Teachers College at Columbia University, a Master of Science in Bilingual Special Education from Bank Street College of Education, and a Bachelor of Science in Elementary Education from The City College of New York. In 2005, she founded the International Leadership Charter High School with the goals of creating a college prep charter high school, that delivers an academically rigorous environment. Dr. Ruíz López's model has resulted in over 95 percent of its scholars graduating within four years and enrolling in the college of their choice. The International Leadership CHS is in its eighteenth year of operation and has received numerous accolades nationally and locally, as the best charter high school in the Bronx. Over the past seven years, the charter school has received national recognition by US NEWS & WORLD REPORT and ranked among its Best High Schools category.

Dr. Ruíz López's vision has expanded to include a middle school that opened in the fall of 2024 and is currently tracking five hundred alumni and postcollege graduates who will take on leadership positions within their communities and institutions. Dr. Ruíz López successfully pursued $22 million in municipal bond financing through Build NYC that led to the completion of a ground-up construction of a twenty-nine-thousand-square-foot three-story school building in the Kingsbridge/Riverdale section of the Bronx. In addition, inspired by the life and work of her childhood pediatrician, Dr. Richard Izquierdo, Dr. Ruíz López collaborated with Urban Health to establish an Adolescent Health and Wellness Center at the charter school to support students with mental health issues.

In 2017, Dr. Ruíz López was one of the recipients of the *Distinguished Women Award (Mujeres Destacadas)* presented by *El Diario*, the largest Spanish daily newspaper organization in the country. In 2022, she was recognized by Attorney General Leticia James and Bronx Borough President Vanessa Gibson as one of the *Power Women of the Bronx*. In 2023 she received the Educator of Excellence Award from the Black Latinx Asian Charter Coalition (BLACC). She is a founding member of the Latino Charter Leaders Roundtable and is its current chair.

(Right) Dr. Elaine Ruíz López, recipient of the BLACC Mosaic Award for Educator of Excellence, June 2023.

(Below, L-R) Bishop Rivera, NYC Chancellor David Banks, Miriam Raccah, Reverend Al Cockfield, Rafiq Kalan Id-din.

Dr. Elaine Ruíz López, recipient of the El Diario Distinguished Woman Award, 2017

Dr. Elaine Ruíz López, recipient of the Power Women of the Bronx Award, June 2022

ACKNOWLEDGEMENTS

First, I would like to thank GOD who placed the vision in my heart to start a school in the Bronx, with a promise to send guardian angels that would take charge over me and to keep me in all my ways. (Psalm 91: 11-12) Thank you for making a way out of no way. I am deeply grateful for the life preservers, the miracles, and the people placed in my life just when I needed them most.

To Anthony "Tony" Lopez my husband, loyal friend, and co-founder, to whom I owe a lifetime of debt and gratitude for walking and fighting alongside me, throughout every moment of this journey for the past eighteen years, believing in my leadership, and supporting the development of my dream and vision even when others said it would not be possible. *Tony, thank you for your patience and for never expecting me to give up the fight to develop a high-performing charter high school that would provide thousands of black and brown adolescents in the Bronx with a quality choice. Although the injustices were at times unbearable, your personal sacrifices have forged a legacy that in the process has changed lives and transformed communities, one scholar at a time.*

I would like to especially thank, Suzanna de Boer, Writing Coach for Forbes Books, who patiently and consistently worked with me closely for 14 months. She ushered me through the writing process, providing thoughtful feedback, and posing questions that would inspire the sharpening of my voice, and use of language for greater clarity in telling my story. *Thank you, Suzanna, for your generosity and for sharing your expertise with me for a stronger manuscript.*

The following colleagues, confidants and friends were part of the village of warriors, who played a significant role in the development of our charter school with great fervor and unparallel commitment. The following amazing human beings and educators also contributed their reflections for inclusion in this book.

I begin here by acknowledging two of the most effective Board Chairs, who also contributed their reflections to some of the chapters found in the Fight for Equity in the Bronx. As board leaders, they maintained a high level of integrity, and loyalty to the mission and governance of the International Leadership Charter High School. Both Dr. John Paul Gonzalez Gutierrez, and Dr. John Rodney Jenkins, demonstrated a superior level of support, oversight, and guidance for every aspect of the school's charter during very challenging years in the charter schools' early journey. *To John Paul, a very special thank you for your endurance during those 8 years of service, and for not walking away when the going got tough.*

The following individuals were alongside me on the front lines of day-to-day operations and figuring things out during the infancy of our charter school. I begin with Robin Calitri, colleague, friend, brilliant educator, and former Principal at South Side High School in the Rockville Centre, Long Island. Alongside his colleagues, he successfully replaced this system of tracking with an honors and college prep sequence that all students would have access to and benefit from.

This International Baccalaureate (IB) high school became a national model of excellence. In 2006, Robin worked as a consultant for our academic program. He mentored me on how to develop and operationalize an accelerated model that was inclusive and would program all students to a Regents Diploma track, and providing all students with access to academic rigor, applying a commonly held belief that "all means all."

Robin selflessly applied his leadership skills and ethical convictions about systemic educational reform, which made our charter school's mission unique and effective in striving for excellence and equity in education. *Thank you, Robin, for stepping in and taking leadership during a tumultuous time in our charter school's history.*

A very special acknowledgment and an abundance of gratitude to Roberta Cummings-Smith, our first Director of Curriculum and Instruction, who accepted the role as Instructional leader by faith, during a time of great uncertainty and what appeared to be insurmountable challenges. *Roberta, thank you for capturing my vision that I wrote for you on a napkin and leading the academic program with grace, unwavering commitment, and strength.*

In 2006 during our first open house at Lehman College, I met a young Dominican Woman and mother, who was in desperate search for a seat at International Leadership Charter High School for her daughter Stephanie. I was taken by her passion, eagerness, and advocacy for her daughter who was selected in the lottery. Edilis Gonzalez was also in search of employment and became my first hire as a school aide. Over the past 18 years, I have watched her grow into a confident professional and today is the very best Director of Parent Engagement and anchor in our school community. *Thank you Edilis for your passion and for taking ownership of our community-grown charter school and protecting its mission-driven purpose over the years.*

Dr. Vashti Acosta, former Chief Executive Officer (CEO) of Amber Charter Schools in the Bronx, the founder of the Latino Charter Leaders Roundtable (LCLR), and a fellow alumnus from Teachers College, Columbia University. Dr. Acosta demonstrated excellence in leadership throughout her tenure at Amber and provided a model of leadership for all Latino-led charter leaders to follow. *Thank you for being a thought partner, the power breakfasts and lunchtime huddles, to support me and all our Latino-led schools.*

Miriam Raccah CEO of BLACC (Black Latinx Asian Charter Collaborative), who took on the monumental task of partnering with Reverend Al Cockfield and others, to lobby the legislature to influence greater support and fiscal equity for our charters, and BLACC-led schools. With her fortitude, perseverance, and a rally cry that representation matters, there has been greater visibility for public charter schools led by people of color. *Miriam, thank you for your reflection and contribution to the Fight for Equity in the Bronx. Education for us, by us!*

Dr. Reverend Alfonso Wyatt, thank you for the book review, your prayers when I have needed them the most, being a role model for our males of color, and your pearls of wisdom spoken at our graduations. *Reverend Wyatt, your inspirational writings and our talks have been a light in the darkness. Thank you for taking the time to write a thoughtful book review.*

A heartfelt recognition to Bishop Raymond Rivera and Marilyn Calo for their steady development of Family Life Academy Charter Schools (FLACS). These two charter school movement pioneers from the Bronx demonstrated that schools of excellence can be successfully led by Latino leaders from within the community and outside of the traditional Charter Management corporate model. *Bishop, thank you for your convictions to support and build community-grown charter schools, as an essential pillar of community control and systemic educational reform. Change is coming and we are the change!*

A very special expression of gratitude to the Parent Leaders who served on the Board to support our charter school over the years to include, Maria Garcia Beltre, Betty Quiroz, Yanelis Munoz, Denise Martinez, Yahaira Dominguez, Darlene Garcia, Doreen Bermudez, Anny Rivas, Addy Rivas, Nubia Moreno, Beatrice Vargas and Virgina Perez.

To the alumni highlighted in the final chapter of the Fight for Equity in the Bronx and those who participated in the special alumni video, lots of love and gratitude for keeping me focused and grounded. *Brandon Aquino, Jailyn Alexis Ruiz, Andrew Rivas, Bryan Molina, Ashley Fernandez, Amelia Almonte, Kiaralys Rivera, Brayhan Morrobel, Ian Bermudez, Triana Bautista, Aissatou Sylla, Dandre Benjamin De Leon, Tuku Gaye, Yocasta Novas Belliard, Marina Bond, Luis Beltre, Joel Beltre, and Isatou Jobateh.*

And to all who have graduated in the past 14 Cohorts, thank you for enriching my life, providing a clear purpose for the fight, and reminding me of *"My Why?" Remember that when a door to your dream does not open easily, be strategic and thoughtful, never give up or give in, simply lean back and kick! God Bless You all.*

A very special expression of gratitude and credit to Joe Conzo, Jr. who granted permission for the use of his original photograph which documented the aftermath of the South Bronx Fires. This photo is featured on the cover of the Fight for Equity in the Bronx: Changing Lives, Transforming Communities one Scholar at a Time. *Joey, thank you for your generosity in providing the amazing photos that depict a few of the most significant and historic struggles that your grandmother, Dr. Evelina Lopez Antonetty, was at the forefront of and is such a crucial part of her legacy. Evelina presente!*

BRONX TIMES

Bronx high school recognized as one of the best in the country

https://www.bxtimes.com/bronx-high-school-recognized-as-one-of-the-best-in-the-country/

NORWOOD NEWS

Norwood: Charter Middle School Opens at former St. Ann Site

https://www.norwoodnews.org/norwood-charter-middle-school-opens-at-former-st-ann-site/

THE RIVERDALE PRESS

International Leadership: We've had enough

https://www.riverdalepress.com/stories/
international-leadership-weve-had-enough,110399

BRONX TIMES

International Leadership Charter School Celebrates 10th Anniversary

https://www.bxtimes.com/international-leadership-charter-school-
celebrates-10th-anniversary/